EASY GLUTEN-FREE, DAIRY-FREE COOKBOOK

EASY
gluten-free,
DAIRY-FREE
COOKBOOK

75 SATISFYING, FUSS-FREE RECIPES

Silvana Nardone

ROCKRIDGE
PRESS

For general information on our other products and services or to obtain technical support, please contact our Customer Care Department within the United States at (866) 744-2665, or outside the United States at (510) 253-0500.

Rockridge Press publishes its books in a variety of electronic and print formats. Some content that appears in print may not be available in electronic books, and vice versa.

TRADEMARKS: Rockridge Press and the Rockridge Press logo are trademarks or registered trademarks of Callisto Media Inc. and/or its affiliates, in the United States and other countries, and may not be used without written permission. All other trademarks are the property of their respective owners. Rockridge Press is not associated with any product or vendor mentioned in this book.

Interior and Cover Designer: Francesca Pacchini
Art Producer: Tom Hood
Editor: Marjorie DeWitt

Photography © Hélène Dujardin, cover and p. 80; Alessio Bogani/Stocksy, p. viii; Leigh Beisch, pp 14, 26; Darren Muir, pp 38, 52, 120; Shea Evans, pp 64, 94; Marija Vidal, p. 104. Food styling by Anna Hampton, cover and p. 80. Author photograph courtesy of Stephen Scott Gross

ISBN: Print 978-1-63807-959-0
eBook 978-1-63807-277-5

R0

{ CONTENTS }

INTRODUCTION

Nowadays, it's fairly common to find that at least one family member has at least one food allergy or intolerance, especially to gluten and/or dairy. Through endless testing, I've developed a way to bring our favorite foods back to the table.

I first joined the gluten-free, dairy-free community after my son, Isaiah, was diagnosed with gluten and dairy intolerance now 14 years ago—back when no one yet knew what gluten even was. It took months for his doctors (and me) to figure out why he was constantly sick with colds and an upset stomach and why he lacked energy seemingly all of the time. To discover that it was gluten and dairy—something I could control—and that by changing his diet he could be better, changed my life. I never looked at food the same way again. Then I learned that millions of Americans are intolerant like Isaiah or have celiac disease, an autoimmune digestive disease that damages the small intestines and prevents nutrient absorption.

From my experiences owning an Italian bakery, running the test kitchen at *Rachael Ray Every Day,* and developing recipes for major magazines like *Food & Wine,* I've absorbed my share of culinary knowledge. Replicating flavors meant reading labels on packages at the supermarket and researching how ingredients could improve texture. Then came testing and more testing in the kitchen until I nailed one recipe after another. Once I had cracked the code on how to re-create textures and flavors that were the same or better than the original, I knew I wanted to help other people cook and bake again.

The truth is that changing our dietary habits isn't easy. We get used to eating whatever we want, whenever we want. When you first eliminate gluten and dairy, all you think about are the foods you can't eat anymore. Once this revelation passes and you start feeling better, a shift happens—and so does your openness to cooking and baking again. You start to feel good. You feel like yourself, and it is a game changer that makes you *want* to eat gluten-free and dairy-free.

Whatever your reason for ditching gluten and dairy—whether you're allergic, intolerant, or just want to improve your health—there are many benefits. If you have a negative reaction when you eat gluten or dairy, your body is trying to tell you something. I'm still amazed that by making changes in our diets, we have the power to help our bodies thrive. Here are three of the most noticeable benefits of being gluten-free and dairy-free:

Stronger Immune System. Since about 80 percent of your immune system is in your gut, anything that upsets your digestion—like gluten and dairy—could disrupt other systems in your body. Translation: removing gluten and dairy from your diet lets your immune system do its job.

Improved Digestion. Cutting out gluten and dairy from your diet can alleviate digestive issues, such as acid reflux and bloating. Plus, if you're lactose intolerant and lack the proper enzymes needed to digest lactose—a natural sugar found in milk—no dairy means common indigestion symptoms like gas, abdominal cramps, nausea, and diarrhea go away.

Clearer Skin. If you have an occasional breakout, eczema, or rashes, eliminating gluten and dairy can make a difference. These skin conditions are your body's response to inflammation. Avoiding gluten and dairy altogether will give your skin a breather.

In this cookbook, you'll love the fast and easy recipes you can make with a limited pantry and basic kitchen tools. Plus, the recipes are familiar favorites made gluten-free and dairy-free, and I've even given you tips throughout the book for ingredient swaps to help with other food sensitivities or to use up what you already have on hand.

Living free of gluten and dairy is a commitment to your health and happiness. Thankfully, cooking and baking gluten-free and dairy-free is easier than you think. The trick is to choose ingredients not just for flavor, but also for performance, so that cake is light and moist, pizza crust is tender and crisp, and gravy is rich and creamy.

Thank you for joining me on your gluten-free, dairy-free journey!

Easy Margherita Pizza
Page 60

Chapter One

GLUTEN-FREE, DAIRY-FREE, AND FUSS-FREE

Sure, gluten-free and dairy-free cooking and baking are easy when it comes to recipes that naturally avoid those ingredients, but why limit yourself? In this cookbook, you'll be making comfort foods and restaurant favorites—no compromises—like Chocolate Chip Banana Bread Loaf (page 35), Easy Margherita Pizza (page 60), Chicken Cacciatore (page 85), and Chocolate Mug Cake (page 102). No need to buy a bunch of unfamiliar, expensive ingredients and tools or put in a ton of work. Instead, with just a limited pantry of accessible ingredients, my time-saving tips, and many recipes that take just 30 minutes or less, you'll have dinner (and dessert) on the table in less time than takeout.

MAKING IT SIMPLE

The first step is to remove all gluten—foods containing wheat, rye, or barley—and dairy—foods made from the milk (and all its derivatives) of animals, including cows, goats, and sheep—from your kitchen. Then, replace your go-to ingredients with easy-to-make (or buy) gluten-free and dairy-free substitutes you *can* eat that look and taste like the originals. This will make going or staying gluten-free and dairy-free easier. Besides gluten-free flours and dairy-free milks, I use ingredients that you probably already have on hand.

Take the pressure off yourself—you don't have to be a gluten-free, dairy-free superhero. Instead of making *all* the basics *all* of the time, get a little help from your supermarket. The reality? Using store-bought dairy-free milk or a gluten-free flour blend means you can spend less time in the kitchen and more time doing what you love, like spending time with family and friends.

THE GLUTEN-FREE PANTRY

Stock your pantry and refrigerator with these gluten-free ingredients, and you'll be ready to cook up all the recipes in this cookbook.

The Gluten-Free Flour Blends

You'll need gluten-free flour to make many of the recipes in this cookbook. I've tested and developed a cup-for-cup substitute for gluten-full all-purpose flour for you to use in the recipes in this cookbook or any recipe that requires flour. I recommend you make my Gluten-Free All-Purpose Flour (page 4) in batches and store it in your pantry so you have it easily on hand when needed. If you already have a gluten-free flour blend that you love in your pantry, go ahead and use that or your favorite store-bought brand.

The Flours and Starches

These days there are many gluten-free flours and starches you can choose from to cook and bake with. This section covers the five essential flours and starches used in this cookbook.

White rice flour: This flour is the main ingredient used in my Gluten-Free All-Purpose Flour (page 4). Combined with tapioca flour, potato starch, salt, and xanthan gum, this makes a one-to-one replacement for traditional flour.

Brown rice flour: Ground from whole-grain brown rice, this flour has a slightly nutty flavor. As with whole wheat flour, if you use too much brown rice flour in a

MY TOP FIVE COMFORT MEALS

Comfort food is important. Our food memories (formed through habits, seasonal influences, travel, restaurant dining, and, of course, our child-hoods) are deeply ingrained in our lives. The truth is that there's no reason why we can't still enjoy ourselves without sacrificing taste and texture. Here is a list of my favorite gluten- and dairy-free comfort food recipes from this cookbook. I know these will satisfy your cravings, as they do mine.

1. **"Fried" Chicken Cutlets** (page 87): This "fried" chicken is healthier and faster to prepare than traditional cutlets because it's baked, not fried. I like to cook the recipe as is or use it to make chicken Parmesan and chicken nuggets.

2. **Spicy Sichuan Beef with Mixed Vegetables** (page 90): This recipe takes me back to my childhood in San Francisco, so it has a special place in my heart. There is no reason to miss out on delicious Chinese flavors when eating gluten- and dairy-free. One taste of this main dish and you'll think you're dining at your favorite Chinese restaurant.

3. **Mexican-Style Stuffed Bell Peppers** (page 84): These cheesy stuffed peppers will make you think you're eating tacos—no tortilla necessary. Another fond memory experience, this recipe reminds me of the stuffed poblano peppers I used to get at one of my favorite Mexican restau-rants in Brooklyn.

4. **Shrimp Fettuccine Alfredo** (page 69): My mother is famous for her creamy pasta sauces, especially her spicy clam sauce. This recipe makes me feel like a kid sitting at the family table. In this twist on her classic fettuccine alfredo recipe, I've stirred in shrimp to make a satisfying one-dish meal.

5. **Crispy Fish Nuggets with Lemon Tartar Sauce** (page 72): This was one of my kids' favorite meals when they were growing up. I used to buy gluten-free fish sticks, but they never quite worked well because the breading would always fall off. With these gluten-free, beer-battered fish nuggets and lemony tartar sauce for dipping, there's no longer a need for store-bought frozen fish sticks.

GLUTEN-FREE ALL-PURPOSE FLOUR

Prep Time: 12 minutes

Nut-Free, Soy-Free, Vegan, 5 Ingredient, 30 Minutes or Less / **Makes About 10 cups**

It took me months of trial and error to create a flour blend that performs cup-for-cup like flour containing gluten. Since then, I've tested a bunch of store-bought flour mixes, and mine still outperforms them in terms of flavor and texture. My flour blend is an old-school mix of white starches, but if you want to add more fiber, you can swap half the white rice flour for brown rice flour. The flour keeps in a cool, dry place or refrigerated for up to 6 months.

6 cups white rice flour

3 cups tapioca flour

1½ cups potato starch

1 tablespoon salt

2 tablespoons xanthan gum

In a large bowl, whisk together the rice flour, tapioca flour, potato starch, salt, and xanthan gum. Transfer the flour to an airtight storage container.

recipe, the finished baked good can be dense. For best results, swap in brown rice flour for up to one-half of the total amount of flour in any recipe.

Almond flour: Made from almonds that are blanched, then ground into a superfine crumb, almond flour adds protein and moisture to recipes.

Potato starch: Not to be confused with potato flour, potato starch (in combination with other starches like tapioca flour) helps yield lighter results, especially in baked goods.

Tapioca flour: Lighter than potato starch, tapioca flour (also known as tapioca starch) is an extract from cassava root. It's the secret to my Gluten-Free All-Purpose Flour (page 4), making for gluten-free baked goods that yield the same texture as their glutenous counterparts.

The Thickeners

These thickeners and binders are used in the recipes to help give body and structure to sauces and salad dressings, as well as to aerate baked goods.

Cornstarch: Cornstarch is the lightest of all starches, making it most similar to gluten-full cake flour. It also acts as a thickener for sauces, pie fillings, puddings, and even dairy-free ice cream like my Snickerdoodle-Pecan Ice Cream (page 103).

Arrowroot: This starch can be used as a substitute for cornstarch as both a thickener and to achieve a light, delicate texture in baked goods, pancakes, and waffles.

Xanthan gum: A binder I've used for more than a decade, xanthan gum is derived from corn. When combined with liquid, it forms a gel-like emulsion that traps bubbles incorporated during the mixing of batters and doughs, resulting in greater aeration. This emulsifier also builds elasticity, replicating gluten-full all-purpose flour properties.

Golden flaxseed meal: Like xanthan gum, fiber-rich flaxseed meal adds body and structure to recipes, and it also gives them a wonderful nuttiness.

THE DAIRY-FREE PANTRY

These are the dairy-free ingredients I use most in my kitchen, either as key ingredients in re-creating dairy-free base recipes or as ingredients in general recipes.

The Milks

For the most part, dairy-free milks are interchangeable; however, these three dairy-free milks perform better in certain recipes given their natural properties:

Cashew milk: This is the most neutral-tasting homemade milk, which is why I use it in many of the recipes. Because of the high-fat content of cashews, this milk has an ultra-creamy texture.

Oat milk: This milk is also neutral in flavor and naturally slightly sweet. If I buy any dairy-free milk in the supermarket, it's refrigerated unsweetened oat milk. Use the recipe for Quick Oat Milk (page 108) if you prefer to make it yourself.

Full-fat coconut milk: I use the solid cream spooned off the top of a refrigerated can of full-fat coconut milk to make luscious and airy Coconut Whipped Cream (page 109).

Other Dairy-Free Essentials

These three ingredients provide dairy-free recipes with much-needed flavor and texture.

Nutritional yeast: This fiber-packed inactive yeast is used in dairy-free cooking as an umami-rich seasoning and delivers a cheesy, nutty flavor. I use it to make essentials in the Homemade Staples chapter, such as Butter (page 106) and "Grated" Parmesan Cheese (page 111).

Tofu: Firm tofu can be used to re-create the texture of cheese, as in Creamy Ricotta (page 112).

Non-hydrogenated shortening: I often prefer to use this vegetable-based fat in baked goods—Chocolate Chip Oatmeal Cookies (page 98) and Chocolate Chip Scones (page 21), for example—in place of dairy-based unsalted butter. It can be substituted in a 1:1 ratio.

MAKE IT WORK: DAIRY-FREE INGREDIENT SWAPS

Throughout the cookbook, I've used specific dairy-free ingredients that you may not have on hand. This chart will help you swap out ingredients and make successful recipes.

DAIRY-FREE INGREDIENT	ALTERNATIVE
Canned coconut milk	Dairy-free unsweetened creamer
Dairy-free buttermilk	Make your own by combining 1 cup dairy-free milk with 1 tablespoon apple cider vinegar. Let the mixture stand for 10 minutes to allow it to activate. Store in the refrigerator in a resealable container for up to 3 days.
Dairy-free cheese	Homemade dairy-free cheese from recipes in *Silvana's Gluten-Free and Dairy-Free Kitchen*. Also, there are plenty of great, meltable dairy-free cheese options at the supermarket, or you can omit cheese entirely from a recipe.
Dairy-free unsweetened creamer	Use the Easy Nut or Seed Milk recipe (page 107), using only 2 cups water.
Non-hydrogenated shortening	Dairy-free buttery sticks
Unsweetened dairy-free milk	You can use any homemade unsweetened dairy-free milk (such as Easy Nut or Seed Milk, page 107) or a store-bought one, preferably without stabilizers or emulsifiers (such as guar gum, xanthan gum, acacia gum, carrageenan, and locust bean gum). In a pinch, you can also use water.

THE ONLY TOOLS YOU'LL NEED

You don't need a bunch of tools to create my recipes, but there are a few items that make things easier. This short list of kitchen tools will make dairy-free cooking and baking fast and simple.

High-speed blender: These blenders are more powerful than the average blender. With motors that have increased horsepower, there's no question you'll get a better outcome, especially when texture is everything. This blender is also a time-saver, since there's no need for a sieve to strain out the little pieces of ingredients that weren't processed by the average blender.

Food processor: I use a food processor for faster produce chopping and to process drier recipes like "Grated" Parmesan Cheese (page 111). I use the blender to make smoother, more liquid-based recipes like dairy-free milks and cheeses, smoothies, and salad dressings.

Immersion blender: This is all you need to transform a soup or sauce from chunky to smooth and creamy—and it takes up less space than a regular blender or food processor.

12-inch balloon whisk: The most important task a whisk performs in my kitchen is aeration. Instead of using a wooden spoon or silicone spatula, I often use a whisk to aerate pancake and cake batters, which makes them lighter in texture.

SMART SHOPPING

If you've just started eating gluten-free and dairy-free, navigating your local grocery store is easier than ever, especially with many national chains manufacturing their own food products. Surprisingly for some people, prices are better than imagined. The key is knowing where to find gluten-free and dairy-free foods in your supermarket and being able to identify which foods are worth buying ready-to-eat and which ones are better made from scratch. Here are five tips for smart shopping success:

1. **Ask customer service where to find gluten-free and dairy-free products.** Sure, you could just walk up and down every aisle—the best way to really get to know a supermarket, and worth the time if you regularly shop at the same store. You can also ask if there's a natural foods section, which usually has shelves stocked with gluten-free and dairy-free goods. Otherwise, some stores have dedicated gluten-free aisles for fast shopping, while others blend in gluten-free products with their gluten-*full* counterparts. The same is true for dairy-free foods, which you're likely to find together in refrigerator display cases.

2. **Shop the perimeter.** That's where you'll find most of the naturally gluten-free and dairy-free foods, like fruit, vegetables, seafood, and meats. If you stop at the deli department, make sure the meats and condiments you select are gluten-free and dairy-free.

3. **Research gluten-free and dairy-free brands before you buy.** If you know what replacement foods you're specifically looking for—like pasta or butter—write them down. Then, do some googling to decide which products look good enough to give them a go. I have included several resources for you to check out in the Resources section at the end of this book.

4. **Ask your Facebook friends or join a gluten-free and dairy-free Facebook group.** There are so many new gluten-free items on the market, but not all of them are worth part of your paycheck. Often, asking friends what gluten-free and dairy-free foods they and their families love is the fastest way to get insight on the best the market has to offer in terms of flavor and cost.

5. **Read labels and look for "gluten-free" and "dairy-free" on packaging.** Reading the ingredients gives you the information you need. Also, look for the allergen disclaimer below the ingredient list to see if a product contains gluten or dairy.

HIDDEN GLUTEN AND DAIRY

Food labels can be confusing, especially when you're new to shopping gluten-free and dairy-free. The solution? When in doubt, check the ingredient label. If you have a gluten or dairy allergy or your gluten or dairy intolerance is severe, this is critical.

When buying packaged and processed foods, look for labels that say "gluten-free," "non-dairy," "dairy-free," and "vegan," which (based on dietary guidelines) means the product will be dairy-free. Better yet, thanks to the US Food & Drug Administration's Food Allergen Labeling and Consumer Protection Act of 2004, food manufacturers are required to declare the eight top allergens, including gluten and dairy. Look for the disclaimer below the ingredient list that states which allergens a product contains.

Contrary to popular belief, "non-dairy" does not actually mean milk-free. According to Alisa Fleming in her article "Non Dairy vs Dairy Free: Why One May Contain Milk," the US Food & Drug Administration (FDA) regulatory definition for non-dairy indicates that a product labeled as such can contain 0.5 percent or less milk by weight. The regulation allows for the presence of milk protein, such as casein, whey, and other dairy derivatives. Casein is the main protein found in milk and cheese, and whey, which is often used in protein powders, is the liquid part of milk that remains once the milk has been curdled and strained. While there is no regulatory definition for "dairy-free," this label is a better indicator of whether a food is dairy-free.

Though it may seem like a no-brainer, it's important to state that foods containing dairy include common ingredients used in cooking and baking, like butter, yogurt, milk, buttermilk, heavy cream, whipping cream, sour cream, condensed milk, and cheese. Look out for less obvious foods that might have dairy. The reality is that packaged and processed foods like chocolate, granola bars, chewing gum, hot dogs, and spice blends can contain dairy.

When you see "gluten-free" on food packaging, the item must comply with the FDA definition of the term, which means the food contains less than 20 parts per million of gluten. Foods can also be certified gluten-free by a third party and will feature the certifier's logo on the packaging.

Although foods like pasta, breads, and waffles obviously have gluten, items like cereal, energy bars, potato chips, and even French fries can also contain gluten. Other foods to look out for include soups, vegan meat substitutes, candy bars, and condiments, such as soy sauce and barbecue sauce.

Some popular hidden ingredients that contain gluten or dairy (and sometimes both) include artificial or natural flavors, deli meats, potato chips, salad dressing, lactic acid starter culture, and prebiotics.

TIME-SAVING TIPS AND TRICKS

Although the recipes in this cookbook are fast and easy, there are some strategies I use to make gluten-free, dairy-free living even better.

Meal Plan

Any plan is better than no plan. If working in restaurant kitchens and owning my own bakery have taught me one thing, it's that that time, energy, and money are what make cooking and baking most efficient. When you're first starting meal planning, start simple. First work with the meals that take less time, have fewer ingredients, and are easier to complete. In the beginning, working with large ingredient lists or complex steps can get discouraging. Build on the basics so things become more second nature to you in the kitchen.

Consider starting with a meal plan for the weekend, then expand to creating one for the week. From there, you can move on to two-week and monthlong plans. To start, create a chart on a piece of paper that lists the days of the week as the column heads. In the rows, list breakfast, lunch, and dinner. In the open squares, list the meal for each day and time. Look closely at the recipes while doing this so you can think about how many people a meal serves and what you can use for leftovers the next day. While charting your meals, you'll quickly notice that many ingredients will be used in more than one recipe. Keep this in mind as you're planning so you purchase the right amount of each item.

After you've completed your plan, go through the recipes and create your shopping list. Be sure to include quantities as you create this list. It's helpful to have a list when going to the grocery store so you can be the most efficient with your time and money.

Prep Ahead

If you're making the homemade staples from chapter 9 or my Gluten-Free All-Purpose Flour (page 4), prep these items in advance so they are readily available. Depending on your needs and the time dairy-free staples will keep in the refrigerator, consider making double batches. The Gluten-Free All-Purpose Flour is perfect for large batches because it can easily be stored in a cool, dry place. There are other recipes in this cookbook that are ideal for doubling and freezing for later use: try White Chicken Chili (page 43), Southwestern Stuffed Sweet Potatoes (page 54), or Meatballs with Spaghetti (page 89).

Make It Easy

Making meal prep fun might require you to adjust your mindset. Rather than thinking about the meals you're planning while at the grocery store, plan ahead and write things down. Apply the same thoroughness and time you apply to things like scheduling your week, budgeting tasks, or solving problems. When you know you have a busy week ahead, plan for it by making meals over the weekend and storing them for the week. Being prepared will help alleviate any potential stress, and it will also make cooking more fun!

Tools

Having your tools in the proper shape is important. Organize your kitchen so you know precisely where things are and won't have to search while you're in the middle of cooking. Your knives should be in proper form, so spend the time to get them sharpened.

Make It Fun

In several of the recipes, I have recommended places where you can add a little something different for a variety of spice, heat, or flavor. Working with this cookbook will give you the knowledge of what to use and why. Use that knowledge to mix things up and try a few new twists. This will make the process more fun!

Health and Convenience

Sure, homemade is best, but for some ingredients store-bought shortcuts are a huge time-saver and almost as good for you as what you'd make yourself. Unfortunately, some dairy-free, gluten-free ingredients, such as nuts, can be expensive. That said, if you can buy nuts in bulk, cost can pretty much be a wash. In this cookbook, you'll find easy recipes for vegan butter, nut and grain milks, whipped cream, and even cream cheese.

DAIRY-FREE FOOD	BRANDS I LIKE	HEALTHIER ALTERNATIVES
Dairy-free butter	Earth Balance, Kite Hill, Miyoko's Creamery	Butter (page 106)
Dairy-free cheese	Kite Hill, Miyoko's Creamery, Violife	Cream Cheese (page 110), Creamy Ricotta (page 112), "Grated" Parmesan Cheese (page 111), Sliceable Tangy Mozzarella (page 113)
Dairy-free ice cream	Ben & Jerry's, Coolhaus, Jeni's, NadaMoo, Van Leeuwen	Snickerdoodle-Pecan Ice Cream (page 103)
Dairy-free milk	Chobani, MALK, New Barn, Oatly	Easy Nut or Seed Milk (page 107), Quick Oat Milk (page 108)
Dairy-free salad dressing	Cleveland Kitchen, Tessaemae's	Cashew Ranch Dressing (page 115), Magic Creamy Cilantro Dressing (page 116)
Gluten-free bread	Canyon Bakehouse, The Gluten-Free Bakery, Little Northern Bakehouse	Sesame Flatbread (page 37), Sliced Sandwich Bread (page 28)

ABOUT THE RECIPES

The recipes in this cookbook include two sets of labels: dietary and ease of use. The dietary labels—Nut-Free, Soy-Free, and Vegan—are allergen-friendly labels that will make it easy to quickly identify potential food sensitivities. In addition, many of the recipes include tips on how to make a recipe allergen-friendly if it's not already identified as such by a label.

The ease-of-use labels—5 Ingredient, 30 Minutes or Less, and One Pot— provide quick insight into the scope and complexity of each recipe. 5 Ingredient tells you that there are five ingredients or fewer (not including olive oil, cooking spray, salt, or pepper), meaning the recipe won't require many steps or items to make it. 30 Minutes or Less specifies that the prep and cook time are no more than 30 minutes total, and One Pot lets you know that the whole recipe can be made from start to finish, including prep, in one pot or pan.

Wholesome Waffles with
Strawberry Compote
Page 24

Chapter Two

BREAKFAST AND BRUNCH

LOADED SWEET POTATO TOAST

Prep Time: 10 minutes **Cook Time:** 15 minutes

Soy-Free, 5 Ingredient, 30 Minutes or Less / **Serves 4**

This recipe is packed with layers of flavor and texture—from the sweetness of the sweet potatoes to the spiciness of the sauce and richness from the avocado. Bonus—it's packed with nutrition, fiber, and antioxidants. Try swapping the sweet potatoes for toasted sourdough bread for the ultimate breakfast sandwich. Or, rather than using the oven, use a toaster or toaster oven to bake the sweet potato toast slices. Just toast for 3 to 4 cycles until the sweet potato is fork-tender.

8 (¼-inch-thick) slices sweet potatoes (about 2 large)

4 tablespoons Creamy Chipotle Sauce (page 117)

2 large avocados, sliced

1 cup baby spinach

8 large eggs, poached or fried

Salt

Freshly ground black pepper

1. Preheat the oven to 400°F. Toast the sweet potato slices directly on an oven rack until golden and fork-tender, about 10 minutes.

2. Divide the sweet potato toast slices among 4 plates. Top each serving with 1 tablespoon Creamy Chipotle Sauce, a quarter of the avocado slices, a quarter of the spinach leaves, 2 eggs, and salt and pepper to taste.

Tip: Slightly undercooking the potatoes initially keeps them from overcooking when you toast them just before serving. To prepare this dish in advance, bake the sweet potato slices until al dente, then refrigerate them for up to 3 days. To serve, just toast the slices until fork-tender before plating and topping them.

ANYTIME SKILLET HASH

Prep Time: 15 minutes **Cook Time:** 20 minutes
Nut-Free, Soy-Free, Vegan, One Pot / **Serves 4**

Serve this hash as a main dish on its own or as a side for everything from breakfast to dinner. I love to serve this with fried eggs. You can store the hash in the refrigerator or freezer, so go ahead and make a double batch for later.

2 tablespoons olive oil

½ medium onion, chopped

2 medium red potatoes, cut into
 ¼-inch cubes

4 garlic cloves, finely chopped

1 bell pepper, seeded and chopped

2 cups kale, stems removed, chopped

1 (15-ounce) can black beans, rinsed
 and drained

½ teaspoon ground cumin

½ teaspoon paprika

Salt

Freshly ground black pepper

¼ cup Magic Creamy Cilantro Dressing
 (page 116), Tex-Mex Style Queso
 (page 118), or store-bought salsa

1. Heat the oil in a large skillet over medium-high heat. Add the onion and potato; cook until golden, about 5 minutes. Add the garlic and bell pepper and cook until softened, about 5 minutes.

2. Add the kale, black beans, cumin, paprika, and salt and pepper to taste. Cover and cook until the kale is wilted. Remove the pan from the heat and drizzle the hash with the sauce.

Tip: Switch up the veggies. Try zucchini, summer squash, sliced mushrooms, or your favorite leafy green, or use whatever you have on hand.

BAKED BERRY CUSTARD OATMEAL

Prep Time: 10 minutes **Cook Time:** 45 minutes

Nut-Free, Soy-Free / **Serves 8**

Baked oatmeal is the perfect all-in-one meal that requires minimal cleanup. This recipe also freezes well, so I like to make a double batch and freeze half either before or after baking. To cut down on the added sugar, I sometimes swap the sugar for 1 mashed banana or 8 chopped dates.

3 cups gluten-free old-fashioned rolled oats

2 large eggs, beaten

½ cup frozen mixed berries

½ cup applesauce

½ cup brown sugar

1 cup unsweetened dairy-free milk

3 tablespoons flaxseed meal

1½ teaspoons baking powder

1½ teaspoons ground cinnamon

1 teaspoon pure vanilla extract

¼ teaspoon salt

1. Preheat the oven to 350°F. In a large bowl, combine the oats, eggs, berries, applesauce, brown sugar, milk, flaxseed meal, baking powder, cinnamon, vanilla, and salt; transfer the mixture to an 8-by-8-inch baking dish.

2. Bake until golden and the liquid is absorbed, about 30 minutes. Serve warm, or let cool, cover, and refrigerate for up to 5 days.

Tip: Line your baking dish with parchment paper and place the portion you want to freeze in a casserole dish with a lid. Freeze until solid, then remove from the pan and wrap tightly with plastic wrap. When you're ready to eat, remove the plastic wrap, pop it into a baking dish, and bake for 45 minutes if uncooked or 10 minutes to warm.

Tip: Swap the berries for your family's favorite fruit, or better yet, place the oat batter into a muffin pan and top each cup with your family's favorite toppings, like blueberries, chopped apples or nuts, or even chocolate chips; bake for 15 minutes.

SHAKSHUKA

Prep Time: 15 minutes **Cook Time:** 35 minutes

Nut-Free, Soy-Free, One Pot / **Serves 6**

Shakshuka is a one-skillet Mediterranean-style dish that uses a flavorful combination of tomatoes, peppers, and spices to gently poach eggs. For faster produce prep, I throw the onion, garlic, jalapeño, and bell pepper into a food processor to finely chop them. For a heartier meal, add a can of rinsed, drained chickpeas or serve with crusty gluten-free bread.

3 tablespoons olive oil

1 medium onion, chopped

1 red bell pepper, stem and ribs removed, finely chopped

4 garlic cloves, finely chopped

1 jalapeño pepper, chopped

1 teaspoon ground cumin

Tabasco

1 (28-ounce) can crushed tomatoes

½ teaspoon salt, plus more for seasoning

¼ teaspoon freshly ground black pepper, plus more for seasoning

6 large eggs

1 tablespoon chopped fresh parsley

2 tablespoons crumbled vegan feta (optional)

1. Heat the olive oil in a large skillet over medium-high heat. Add the onion, bell pepper, garlic, and jalapeño pepper and cook until softened and golden, about 5 minutes. Stir in the cumin, Tabasco to taste, tomatoes, ½ teaspoon salt, and ¼ teaspoon pepper. Increase the heat to high and bring the mixture to a simmer; cook until thickened, about 15 minutes.

2. Make 6 wells in the sauce and crack an egg into each one; season with salt and pepper and reduce the heat to medium-low. Cover and cook until the egg whites are set but yolks are still runny, another 8 minutes. To serve, sprinkle with the parsley and the feta (if using).

Tip: For family members who prefer yolks firm, cook for 10 to 12 minutes. For less spiciness, omit the jalapeño pepper and Tabasco.

Tip: This recipe can be prepared ahead of time. Make the sauce and refrigerate it. When you're ready to eat, reheat the tomato mixture, make the wells, crack the eggs on top, and cook until they're set.

HAM, QUESO, AND BROCCOLI QUICHE CUPS

Prep Time: 10 minutes **Cook Time:** 20 minutes
Nut-Free, Soy-Free, 30 Minutes or Less / **Makes 12 quiche cups**

These quiche cups—crispy hash-brown crusts filled with fluffy eggs—are completely customizable, so go ahead and use whatever veggies you have on hand. They also make a fast-and-easy, grab-and-go meal for busy weekdays. For extra flavor, drizzle with Magic Creamy Cilantro Dressing (page 116) or top with hot sauce.

Nonstick cooking spray

1 (12-ounce) bag frozen hash browns

1½ cups (about 12 ounces) fresh or frozen
    broccoli florets, cut into bite-size pieces

6 large eggs

¼ cup Tex-Mex Style Queso (page 118)

½ cup finely chopped deli ham

½ cup unsweetened dairy-free milk

¼ teaspoon salt

1 teaspoon mustard

½ teaspoon garlic powder

2 tablespoons finely chopped fresh parsley

¼ cup chopped scallions

1. Preheat the oven to 425°F. Grease a 12-cup muffin pan with nonstick cooking spray or line it with muffin liners.

2. Put 2 tablespoons of hash browns in each muffin cup; press them evenly across the bottom and up the sides. Divide the broccoli evenly among the muffin cups.

3. In a medium bowl, whisk the eggs. Stir in the Tex-Mex Style Queso, ham, milk, salt, mustard, garlic powder, and parsley.

4. Pour ¼ cup of the egg mixture into each muffin cup until about ¾ full; sprinkle each cup with scallions. Bake until the filling is set and the top is light golden brown, about 20 minutes.

Tip: Swap in ½ cup of your favorite shredded dairy-free cheese for the Tex-Mex Style Queso.

CHOCOLATE CHIP SCONES

Prep Time: 15 minutes **Cook Time:** 25 minutes
Nut-Free, Soy-Free / **Makes 8 scones**

In our gluten-full days, my family and I would bike to a little bakery in Brooklyn every Sunday for the lightest, most flavor-packed scones. The trick to getting those flaky layers is in the technique used in cutting the dough. Using a sharp knife, cut straight down with no sawing action for the best results.

1¼ cups cold store-bought dairy-free creamer, plus more for brushing

2 teaspoons apple cider vinegar

2 cups Gluten-Free All-Purpose Flour (page 4) or store-bought blend

2 tablespoons granulated sugar, plus more for sprinkling

1 tablespoon baking powder

¼ teaspoon baking soda

½ teaspoon salt

6 tablespoons shortening or dairy-free buttery sticks, frozen and cut into ½-inch pieces

1 large egg, cold and lightly beaten

1 cup dairy-free chocolate chips

1. Preheat the oven to 375°F with a rack in the middle. Line a baking sheet with parchment paper.

2. In a small bowl, whisk together the creamer and vinegar.

3. In a large bowl, whisk together the flour, sugar, baking powder, baking soda, and salt. Cut in the shortening with a fork until coarse crumbs form. Add the creamer mixture, eggs, and chocolate chips; stir with a fork to combine.

4. Pat out the dough to form a ½-inch-thick round. Cut the round into 8 triangles and place them about 2 inches apart on the prepared baking sheet. Brush each triangle with creamer and sprinkle each generously with sugar. Bake until golden and puffed, about 25 minutes. Let cool on a wire rack.

Tip: For a less-sweet variation, reduce the sugar to 1 teaspoon, omit the chocolate chips, and sprinkle the dough with sugar before baking. Or for a savory version, omit the sugar and the chocolate chips and add ¾ cup crumbled cooked bacon, ¾ cup store-bought dairy-free shredded cheddar cheese, and 1 tablespoon chopped chives.

CHICKPEA PANCAKES WITH MAPLE YOGURT TOPPING AND BERRIES

Prep Time: 15 minutes **Cook Time:** 20 minutes
Nut-Free, Soy-Free, Vegan / **Serves 4**

My family loves waking up on the weekends to the sweet smell of pancakes hot off the griddle. These pancakes are great for breakfast, lunch, or dinner. Made with protein-rich chickpea flour, they will fuel you all day long.

For the pancakes

1 cup chickpea flour

½ cup potato starch

2½ teaspoons baking powder

¼ teaspoon salt

2 large eggs

1 cup unsweetened dairy-free milk

2 tablespoons olive oil

1 tablespoon pure maple syrup

1 tablespoon distilled white vinegar

Nonstick cooking spray

For the topping

1 cup dairy-free plain or vanilla yogurt

2 tablespoons pure maple syrup

¼ teaspoon ground cinnamon

1 cup fresh berries, such as blueberries, raspberries, or chopped strawberries

To make the pancakes:

1. In a large bowl, combine the chickpea flour, potato starch, baking powder, and salt.

2. In a small bowl, whisk together the eggs, milk, oil, maple syrup, and vinegar. Pour the egg mixture over the flour mixture and stir until just combined; let stand for 5 minutes.

3. Heat a large nonstick skillet over medium heat and lightly grease it with cooking spray. Reduce the heat to medium-low. Pour the batter about ¼ cup at a time into the skillet and cook the pancakes until golden and set, about 2 minutes on each side. Repeat with the remaining batter.

To make the topping:

4. In a small bowl, whisk together the yogurt, maple syrup, and cinnamon. Serve the pancakes with the yogurt topping and fresh berries.

....

Tip: No chickpea flour? Swap in 1 cup of almond flour, which provides protein and fiber along with an extra dose of healthy fats.

WHOLESOME WAFFLES WITH STRAWBERRY COMPOTE

Prep Time: 15 minutes **Cook Time:** 20 minutes
Nut-Free, Soy-Free / **Serves 6**

One of our family's favorite traditions is to make waffles on the weekends. My kids drown their waffles in maple syrup, while my husband and I love them with strawberry compote. For a new dessert idea, enjoy the compote over dairy-free ice cream.

For the strawberry compote

1 pint (16 ounces) strawberries, hulled
   and chopped
¼ cup water

2 tablespoons honey or maple syrup
1 teaspoon freshly squeezed lemon juice

For the waffles

Nonstick cooking spray
2 cups plus 1 tablespoon Gluten-Free
   All-Purpose Flour (page 4) or
   store-bought blend
1 tablespoon baking powder
½ teaspoon salt

1½ cups unsweetened dairy-free milk
6 tablespoons dairy-free butter, melted
¼ cup pure maple syrup
1 tablespoon pure vanilla extract
2 large eggs, separated, plus 2 egg whites

To make the strawberry compote:

1. Put the strawberries, water, and honey in a small saucepan and bring the mixture to a simmer over medium heat. Cook until thickened, about 7 minutes. Stir in the lemon juice and transfer the compote to a bowl. Let it cool slightly.

To make the waffles:

2. Lightly grease a waffle iron with nonstick cooking spray. Preheat the iron according to the manufacturer's directions.

3. In a large bowl, whisk together the flour blend, baking powder, and salt.

4. In a medium bowl, whisk together the milk, butter, maple syrup, vanilla, and 2 egg yolks. Stir the liquid mixture into the flour mixture until just combined.

5. In the bowl of an electric mixer, beat the 4 egg whites on high until soft peaks form. Gently fold the beaten egg whites into the waffle batter, working in three batches, until just combined.

6. Pour ½ cup of the batter onto the preheated waffle iron and cook until golden brown and crisp. Serve with the strawberry compote.

Tip: To store, place cooled waffles in a resealable bag and refrigerate for up to 1 week or freeze for up to 1 month.

Olive and Herb
Focaccia Bread
Page 32

Chapter Three

BREAD AND BAKED GOODS

SLICED SANDWICH BREAD

Prep Time: 10 minutes, plus 30 minutes to rise **Cook Time:** 55 minutes
Nut-Free, Soy-Free / **Makes 1 loaf (10 slices)**

This no-fuss sandwich bread is easy and versatile, and it can be used for other things besides sandwiches; try it for French toast, croutons, or even breadcrumbs.

1½ cups warm water

3 tablespoons pure maple syrup

1 (¼-ounce) packet active dry yeast

1½ cups brown rice flour

1½ cups Gluten-Free All-Purpose Flour
  (page 4) or store-bought blend

1 tablespoon baking powder

1 teaspoon salt

¼ cup olive oil

2 teaspoons apple cider vinegar

1. Line a 9-by-5-inch loaf pan with parchment paper, leaving a 2-inch overhang.

2. In a small bowl, combine the warm water and maple syrup. Stir in the yeast until it is dissolved and set the bowl aside.

3. In a large bowl or stand mixer, mix together the brown rice flour, flour blend, baking powder, and salt. Add the yeast mixture, and while beating on low speed, slowly stream in the oil, then the vinegar; mix until a dough forms. Transfer the dough to the prepared pan and let it proof for 30 minutes.

4. Meanwhile, preheat the oven to 375°F. Bake the bread for 45 minutes, then cover it with foil and bake until golden brown or the internal temperature reaches 200°F, about 8 minutes more. Let the bread cool in the pan for 5 minutes, then carefully transfer it to a wire rack to cool completely, about 2 hours.

Tip: Once it has cooled, slice the loaf and place it in a resealable plastic bag. Store the bread at room temperature for up to 5 days, or freeze it for up to 3 months.

BISCUITS

Prep Time: 15 minutes **Cook Time:** 15 minutes
Nut-Free, Soy-Free, 30 Minutes or Less / **Makes 8 biscuits**

Go ahead and smother these tender biscuits in gravy, toast and spread them with butter and jam, or serve them plain as a side for holiday feasts and brunches. These biscuits are best served warm. You can reheat them in the microwave on high for 5 to 10 seconds. Store the biscuits at room temperature in a resealable bag for up to 2 days.

2 cups Gluten-Free All-Purpose Flour (page 4) or store-bought blend, plus more for dusting

1½ tablespoons baking powder

½ teaspoon salt

½ cup dairy-free buttery sticks, cold

1 large egg, beaten

⅔ cup unsweetened dairy-free milk

1 tablespoon pure maple syrup

2 teaspoons apple cider vinegar

1. Preheat the oven to 450°F. Line a baking sheet with parchment paper.

2. In a large bowl, combine the flour blend, baking powder, and salt. Cut in the buttery sticks with a fork until coarse crumbs form. Stir in the egg, milk, maple syrup, and vinegar; mix to combine.

3. Place a piece of parchment paper on a clean, dry surface and dust it lightly with flour. Using lightly floured hands or a rolling pin, roll out the dough evenly to a ¾-inch thickness. Using a biscuit cutter, cut the dough into rounds and place the rounds on the prepared baking sheet. Reshape the scraps of dough and repeat cutting dough rounds to make 8 biscuits.

4. Bake the biscuits until golden brown, about 12 minutes. Let them cool for 5 minutes, then serve warm.

....

Tip: Brush the biscuits with melted butter before baking for a nice sheen and more browning (translation: more flavor!).

"CHEESY" CRACKERS

Prep Time: 10 minutes, plus 30 minutes to chill **Cook Time:** 15 minutes

Soy-Free, Vegan, 5 Ingredient / **Makes about 40 crackers**

When I couldn't find a gluten-free cracker that I loved at the supermarket, I started baking my own. Nutritional yeast—an inactive form of yeast grown and harvested from molasses—is a great substitute for a pop of cheesy flavor.

2 tablespoons flaxseed meal

1 ¾ cups almond flour

¼ cup nutritional yeast

½ teaspoon salt

¼ cup melted coconut oil

Nonstick cooking spray

1. In a small bowl, whisk together the flaxseed meal and 4 tablespoons water; let this mixture sit for at least 10 minutes.

2. In a large bowl or stand mixer, mix together the almond flour, nutritional yeast, and salt. Add the flaxseed mixture and mix on low speed, slowly streaming in the oil until a crumbly dough forms. Gather the dough into a ball, wrap the ball tightly in plastic wrap, and refrigerate it for 30 minutes.

3. Preheat the oven to 350°F. Line two baking sheets with parchment paper.

4. Place the ball of dough between two sheets of parchment paper and, using a rolling pin, roll out the dough evenly to about ¼ inch thickness. Using a greased pizza cutter, cut the dough into 2-inch squares. Using a greased spatula, carefully transfer each cracker to the prepared baking sheets, spacing the crackers about ¼ inch apart. Bake for 15 minutes, turning the pans halfway through for even cooking.

5. Let the crackers cool slightly on the baking sheets, about 5 minutes, then transfer them to a wire rack to cool completely.

Tip: Place the crackers in a resealable bag and store them at room temperature for up to 1 month.

PUMPKIN QUICK BREAD

Prep Time: 15 minutes **Cook Time:** 50 minutes
Nut-Free, Soy-Free / **Makes 1 loaf (10 to 12 slices)**

This light, moist pumpkin loaf cake is cozy with warm spices. Prefer single-serve portions? Use this recipe to make muffins instead. Check the bread in the last 10 minutes of baking, and tent it loosely with foil if it is over-browning.

1⅓ cups Gluten-Free All-Purpose Flour
  (page 4) or store-bought blend
2 teaspoons baking powder
1 teaspoon ground nutmeg
1 teaspoon ground cinnamon

1 teaspoon salt
1 (15-ounce) can pure pumpkin puree
1 cup packed light brown sugar
4 large eggs

1. Preheat the oven to 350°F. Line a 9-by-5-inch loaf pan with parchment paper, leaving a 2-inch overhang.

2. In a medium bowl, combine the flour blend, baking powder, nutmeg, cinnamon, and salt.

3. In the bowl of an electric mixer, beat together the pumpkin puree and sugar on medium speed until blended. Beat in the eggs until combined. On low speed, mix in the flour mixture in three additions, beating until just combined; transfer the batter to the prepared pan.

4. Bake until the bread is golden and a toothpick inserted in the center comes out clean, about 50 minutes. Let cool on a wire rack for 20 minutes, then remove the bread from the pan and let it cool completely before slicing.

Tip: Store the loaf whole, wrapped in foil lined with wax paper. Once it's been sliced, store the bread at room temperature in a resealable container for up to 3 days or freeze the foil-wrapped loaf or slices in a resealable bag for up to 3 months.

OLIVE AND HERB FOCACCIA BREAD

Prep Time: 45 minutes, plus 1 hour 45 minutes to rise **Cook Time:** 25 minutes

Nut-Free, Soy-Free / **Serves 8**

Don't be alarmed by the amount of extra-virgin olive oil in this recipe. Not only is it heart healthy, it's also the key to the focaccia bread's crisp, flavorful crust.

12 tablespoons extra-virgin olive oil, plus
 more for greasing, divided

4½ teaspoons instant dry yeast

1 cup lukewarm water

4½ cups Gluten-Free All-Purpose Flour
 (page 4) or store-bought blend

1½ tablespoons xanthan gum

2 teaspoons salt

4 large eggs

1 cup unsweetened dairy-free milk

2 teaspoons apple cider vinegar

24 green or black olives, pitted and chopped

2 teaspoons chopped fresh rosemary

2 teaspoons chopped fresh thyme

Grated zest of 1 large lemon
 (about 1 teaspoon)

Kosher salt (optional)

1. Grease a large bowl with oil. Line a 12-by-18-inch baking pan with parchment paper.

2. In a small bowl, dissolve the yeast in the water. Stir with a fork until the yeast is dissolved; let it stand until foamy and activated, about 5 minutes.

3. In a large bowl, combine the flour blend, xanthan gum, and salt.

4. In a medium bowl, whisk together the eggs, milk, 2 tablespoons of oil, and the vinegar; stir the egg mixture into the flour mixture. Stir in the activated yeast and continue to "knead" the dough with a spatula for about 10 minutes. The dough will be sticky.

5. Place the dough in the prepared bowl, turning to coat it with oil. Cover the bowl with plastic wrap and set it in a warm, draft-free place to rise until doubled in size, about 1½ hours.

6. Pour 5 tablespoons of oil in the prepared baking pan. Place the dough in the center of the pan. If necessary, sprinkle the dough with flour to make handling it easier. Using your fingertips, press out the dough into a 13-by-10-inch rectangle; let it rest for 10 minutes.

7. Top the dough with the olives, rosemary, thyme, and lemon zest. Drizzle the remaining 5 tablespoons of oil evenly over the top; cover the pan with plastic wrap and let the dough proof for 25 minutes.

8. Preheat the oven to 475°F. Using your fingertips, press the dough all over to make indentions; bake until the focaccia is golden brown and the edges are crusty, 20 to 25 minutes. Sprinkle with kosher salt, if using, and cut into pieces.

Tip: Store the focaccia in a resealable bag at room temperature for up to 3 days or in the refrigerator for up to 1 week. Reheat in the microwave for 10 seconds before serving.

ORANGE-CRANBERRY BREAD

Prep Time: 30 minutes, plus 20 minutes to rest **Cook Time:** 1 hour 10 minutes
Soy-Free, Vegan / **Makes 1 loaf (10 to 12 slices)**

I like to serve this comforting, orange-scented cranberry loaf with a cup of English breakfast tea as part of my Thanksgiving brunch. Check the bread in the last 10 minutes of baking, and tent it loosely with foil if it is over-browning.

½ cup granulated sugar

Zest and juice of 1 orange
   (about 3 tablespoons each)

1 cup almond flour

¾ cup brown rice flour

¼ cup tapioca flour

1 teaspoon baking powder

½ teaspoon baking soda

¼ teaspoon salt

¾ cup full-fat coconut milk

2 tablespoons pure maple syrup

½ teaspoon orange extract (optional)

½ teaspoon pure vanilla extract

½ to 1 cup fresh cranberries, thawed if
   frozen and preferably halved

1. Preheat the oven to 350°F and line a 9-by-5-inch loaf pan with parchment paper, leaving a 2-inch overhang.

2. In a large bowl, combine the granulated sugar and orange zest. Use your fingers or the back of a spoon to release the orange oils until the sugar is fragrant, about 30 seconds. Stir in the almond flour, brown rice flour, tapioca flour, baking powder, baking soda, and salt.

3. In a small bowl, whisk together the orange juice, coconut milk, maple syrup, orange extract (if using), and vanilla. Add the orange juice mixture to the flour mixture and whisk until a batter forms; fold in the cranberries.

4. Transfer the batter to the prepared loaf pan.

5. Bake the bread until golden brown and a toothpick inserted in the center comes out clean, about 1 hour. Let it cool completely in the pan for at least 2 hours before slicing.

Tip: Wrap the loaf or individual slices in plastic wrap and store the bread at room temperature for up to 4 days.

CHOCOLATE CHIP BANANA BREAD LOAF

Prep Time: 15 minutes **Cook Time:** 50 minutes
Nut-Free, Soy-Free / **Makes 1 loaf (10 to 12 slices)**

Warm your day with cozy vanilla and cinnamon baked into a banana-sweetened bread loaded with chocolate chips. This quick bread makes the perfect breakfast, snack, or even dessert.

3 ripe bananas
2 cups Gluten-Free All-Purpose Flour
   (page 4) or store-bought blend
1 tablespoon baking powder
1 teaspoon ground cinnamon
½ teaspoon salt

2 large eggs
⅔ cup pure maple syrup
½ cup dairy-free plain yogurt
1 tablespoon pure vanilla extract
1 cup dairy-free mini chocolate
   chips, divided

1. Preheat the oven to 350°F and line a 9-by-5-inch loaf pan with parchment paper, leaving a 2-inch overhang.

2. In a small bowl, mash the bananas with a fork.

3. In a medium bowl, combine the flour blend, baking powder, cinnamon, and salt.

4. In the bowl of an electric mixer, beat together the eggs, maple syrup, yogurt, and vanilla on medium speed until combined. Add the mashed bananas; beat until combined. Reduce the speed to low, and gradually beat in the flour mixture until just combined; fold in ¾ cup of the chocolate chips. Transfer the batter to the prepared pan and sprinkle the remaining ¼ cup chocolate chips over the top.

5. Bake the bread until the top is golden and a toothpick inserted in the center comes out clean, about 50 minutes. Let it cool on a wire rack for 20 minutes, then remove the bread from the pan and let it cool completely before slicing.

Tip: Stir ½ cup of your favorite nut, like walnuts or pecans, into the batter for a nice crunch.

BLUEBERRY OATMEAL MUFFINS

Prep Time: 10 minutes **Cook Time:** 20 minutes

Soy-Free, 30 Minutes or Less / **Makes 12 muffins**

These light and fluffy muffins are bursting with blueberry and lemon flavor—and a heart-healthy dose of fiber. I like to make these on the weekends for an easy weekday breakfast or quick snack.

1 cup Gluten-Free All-Purpose Flour (page 4) or store-bought blend

1 cup gluten-free old-fashioned rolled oats

1 teaspoon baking powder

½ teaspoon baking soda

¾ teaspoon salt

2 large eggs

⅔ cup pure maple syrup

½ cup dairy-free plain yogurt

¼ cup coconut oil, melted

¼ cup unsweetened dairy-free milk

1 teaspoon grated lemon zest

1 teaspoon pure vanilla extract

1 cup fresh blueberries

1. Preheat the oven to 350°F and line a muffin pan with paper liners.

2. In a large bowl, whisk together the flour, oats, baking powder, baking soda, and salt.

3. In a medium bowl, whisk together the eggs, maple syrup, yogurt, oil, milk, lemon zest, and vanilla until combined. Fold the egg mixture into the flour mixture until just combined. Gently fold in the blueberries.

4. Evenly divide the mixture among the prepared muffin cups and bake until golden and a toothpick inserted in the center of a muffin comes out clean, about 20 minutes. Remove the muffins from the pan and let them cool completely on a wire rack.

Tip: No fresh blueberries? Use frozen blueberries without thawing to avoid discoloring the batter.

SESAME FLATBREAD

Prep Time: 10 minutes **Cook Time:** 20 minutes

Nut-Free, Vegan, 30 Minutes or Less / **Makes 6 flatbreads**

This flatbread was inspired by naan, a yeasted flatbread that incorporates yogurt into the dough. The yogurt, which is fermented, gives the bread acidity, making it tender and fluffy.

3½ cups Gluten-Free All-Purpose Flour
  (page 4) or store-bought blend
1½ teaspoons salt
1¼ to 1½ cups lukewarm water (65°F)

⅓ cup unsweetened dairy-free plain yogurt,
  at room temperature
3 tablespoons olive oil
2 tablespoons sesame seeds, for sprinkling

1. In a large bowl, whisk together the flour and salt. Add 1¼ cups water and the yogurt and olive oil. Stir to combine.

2. If the dough seems too dry, add the remaining ¼ cup water, 1 tablespoon at a time, until the dough is soft and pliable, and then let the dough sit for 3 minutes to thicken.

3. Dust a clean work surface with flour and transfer the dough onto it. Using floured hands, knead the dough until smooth and elastic, about 1 minute.

4. Divide the dough into 6 equal pieces. Sprinkle the work surface with about 1 teaspoon of sesame seeds and, using a rolling pin, roll out 1 piece of dough on top of the sesame seeds into an oval about 10 inches long, 8 inches wide, and ⅓ inch thick.

5. Set a dry cast-iron skillet over medium heat. Place the dough oval into the hot pan and cook, turning once, until char marks appear on the bottom, about 3 minutes. Transfer the cooked flatbread to a baking sheet. Repeat the rolling and cooking process with the remaining dough pieces.

Tip: If you prefer to bake these in the oven, place an inverted baking sheet on the bottom rack of the oven and preheat the oven to 475°F. A few minutes before baking, lightly spray the dough rounds with water and place them on a sheet of parchment paper. Transfer them with the paper to the inverted baking sheet, and bake until lightly golden, about 3 minutes.

Thai-Inspired Coconut
Soup with Ginger
and Lime
Page 44

Chapter Four

SOUPS AND SALADS

FOUR BEAN SALAD

Prep Time: 10 minutes, plus 1 hour to chill

Nut-Free, Soy-Free, Vegan, One Pot / **Serves 6**

This cold bean salad only gets better the longer it marinates and keeps well in the refrigerator for up to five days, so it's perfect for making ahead of time. While the tarragon-infused vinegar adds complexity to the salad, you can also just add more red wine vinegar.

2 garlic cloves, finely chopped

2 tablespoons granulated sugar

1 tablespoon Italian seasoning

¼ cup tarragon vinegar

¼ cup red wine vinegar

¼ cup olive oil

½ teaspoon salt

¼ teaspoon freshly ground black pepper

1 (15.5-ounce) can red kidney beans, rinsed and drained

1 (15.5-ounce) can chickpeas, rinsed and drained

1 (15.5-ounce) can lima beans, rinsed and drained

1 (12-ounce) bag frozen cut green beans, thawed

½ medium red onion, chopped

½ large bell pepper, chopped

1. In a large bowl, whisk together the garlic, sugar, Italian seasoning, tarragon vinegar, red wine vinegar, olive oil, salt, and pepper to combine.

2. Add the kidney beans, chickpeas, lima beans, green beans, onion, and bell pepper to the bowl; stir to coat all the beans well. Cover and refrigerate the salad for at least 1 hour; serve chilled or at room temperature.

Tip: Short on time? Swap in your favorite vinaigrette in place of the homemade dressing.

LEMONY LENTIL AND KALE SOUP

Prep Time: 10 minutes **Cook Time:** 25 minutes

Nut-Free, Soy-Free, Vegan, One Pot / **Serves 4**

This satisfying soup cooks up in less than 30 minutes—the solution to a fast and easy weeknight meal. Dry lentils cook in as little as 15 minutes, making them perfect for busy weeknights. Want an even heartier meal? Add four sliced precooked sausages to the pot with the chopped onion and celery.

3 tablespoons olive oil

1 large onion, chopped

1 stalk celery, chopped

1 large carrot, chopped

4 garlic cloves, finely chopped

1 bay leaf

1 teaspoon ground coriander

1 teaspoon ground cumin

1 teaspoon curry powder

½ teaspoon salt

½ teaspoon freshly ground black pepper

2 tablespoons tomato paste

2 cups chopped kale

5 cups store-bought vegetable broth

1 cup dry red lentils

½ lemon

Chopped cilantro, for topping

1. In a large pot, heat the olive oil over medium-high heat. Stir in the onion, celery, carrot, garlic, and bay leaf. Cook until browned, about 5 minutes.

2. Stir in the coriander, cumin, curry powder, salt, and pepper; cook until fragrant, about 2 minutes more.

3. Stir in the tomato paste, kale, broth, and lentils; cover and simmer over medium heat until the lentils are tender, about 20 minutes. Season with salt to taste. To serve, squeeze the lemon over each bowl of soup and top with cilantro.

Tip: Heat things up by stirring in some chopped jalapeño pepper or a splash of Tabasco before serving.

BRAZILIAN-STYLE FISH STEW

Prep Time: 10 minutes **Cook Time:** 30 minutes
Soy-Free, One Pot / **Serves 6**

When I want minimal cleanup and an all-in-one meal, stews are my go-to. I like to serve this stew over rice or quinoa, but it can also be spooned over cooked spaghetti squash or even wilted greens. This recipe is versatile, which makes it ideal for using up what's already in your refrigerator or freezer.

2 tablespoons olive oil

1 tablespoon ground cumin

1 tablespoon paprika

4 garlic cloves, finely chopped

2 onions, chopped

3 large bell peppers, chopped

1½ pounds skinless cod fillets, cut into
    1-inch pieces

1 (16-ounce) can diced tomatoes, drained

1 (16-ounce) can coconut milk

Juice of 4 limes (about
    6 tablespoons), divided

1 teaspoon salt

1 teaspoon freshly ground black pepper

1 bunch fresh cilantro, chopped

3 cups cooked rice

Red pepper flakes (optional)

1. Heat the olive oil in a large pot over medium-high heat. Add the cumin, paprika, and garlic and cook, stirring, until fragrant, about 1 minute. Add the onions and bell peppers and cook until softened, about 5 minutes. Add the fish, tomatoes, coconut milk, 2 tablespoons of the lime juice, salt, and pepper. Cover the pot, reduce the heat to low, and simmer, stirring occasionally, for 15 minutes.

2. Stir in three-quarters of the cilantro and the remaining 4 tablespoons lime juice; cook until the fish is completely cooked through, about 5 minutes more. Season the soup with salt and pepper to taste.

3. Divide the rice among 6 serving bowls, and ladle the soup over the rice. To serve, top with the remaining cilantro and the red pepper flakes (if using).

Tip: You can make this stew in your slow cooker. Just place all the ingredients except the rice, cilantro, and optional red pepper flakes in the slow cooker and cook on low for 6 to 8 hours. Serve over cooked rice and top with cilantro and red pepper flakes (if using).

WHITE CHICKEN CHILI

Prep Time: 20 minutes **Cook Time:** 30 minutes
Soy-Free, One Pot / **Serves 8**

My dairy-free chicken chili is creamy, cheesy, and just as comforting as the original. To cut down on prep time, substitute 2 teaspoons garlic powder for the garlic cloves. I love making a double batch of this soup and freezing half of it in a large freezer-safe resealable container for up to 3 months.

2 tablespoons olive oil

2 medium yellow onions, chopped

4 garlic cloves, finely chopped

1 poblano pepper, stemmed, seeded, and chopped

1 tablespoon ground cumin

2 tablespoons dried oregano

1 tablespoon freshly ground black pepper

4 medium chicken breasts, cut into 1-inch pieces

1 teaspoon salt

4 (15.5-ounce) cans low-sodium pinto beans, rinsed and drained

24 ounces store-bought chicken broth

2 (7-ounce) cans fire-roasted chopped green chiles

2 cups full-fat coconut milk

Juice of 1 lemon

1 cup shredded dairy-free mozzarella, for topping (optional)

1 cup crushed tortilla chips, for topping (optional)

1. Heat the oil in a large pot over medium-high heat. Add the onions, garlic, poblano pepper, cumin, oregano, and black pepper. Cook until the onions are softened, about 5 minutes. Stir in the chicken and salt; cook until the meat is cooked through, about 5 minutes.

2. Stir in the beans, broth, and green chiles; bring the soup to a boil, then reduce the heat to low and simmer for 30 minutes.

3. Stir in the coconut milk and lemon juice and return the soup to a simmer; then remove the pot from the heat. Serve with the shredded mozzarella and crushed tortilla chips (if using).

Tip: Make the chili less spicy by omitting the poblano pepper and using just 1 can green chiles.

THAI-INSPIRED COCONUT SOUP WITH GINGER AND LIME

Prep Time: 10 minutes **Cook Time:** 20 minutes
Soy-Free, Vegan, 30 Minutes or Less, One Pot / **Serves 8**

Made fragrant with ginger, lime zest, and cilantro, this recipe is a vegan, keto-friendly version of traditional Thai soup.

8 cups store-bought vegetable broth

1-inch piece fresh ginger, peeled and finely chopped

2 garlic cloves, finely chopped

1 teaspoon lime zest

1 cup full-fat coconut cream

1 cup sliced mushrooms

1 tomato, chopped

½ yellow onion, chopped

1 cup chopped broccoli

1 cup chopped cauliflower

1 cup chopped fresh cilantro, for topping

1 lime, cut into wedges

In a large pot, bring the broth, ginger, garlic, and lime zest to a simmer over medium heat. Stir in the coconut cream, mushrooms, tomato, onion, broccoli, and cauliflower and cook until the vegetables are tender. To serve, top each serving with cilantro and a lime wedge.

....

Tip: Make it a meal by stirring in cubed firm tofu or cooked shrimp.

ROASTED GARLIC AND MUSHROOM SOUP

Prep Time: 20 minutes **Cook Time:** 40 minutes
Nut-Free, Soy-Free, Vegan / **Serves 4 to 6**

This is my dairy-free alternative to the classic condensed cream of mushroom soup I grew up eating. The roasted garlic adds a nice flavor boost. My trick to getting it nice and creamy? I add potato to the soup to give it body and make the consistency more bisque-like. Add ½ cup more broth or creamer if you prefer your soup thinner.

20 ounces button mushrooms, wiped clean, stems trimmed
½ large onion, quartered
3 garlic cloves, unpeeled
4 sprigs fresh rosemary
3 tablespoons olive oil

½ teaspoon salt
½ teaspoon freshly ground black pepper
1 quart store-bought vegetable broth
1 russet potato, peeled and cut into ½-inch pieces

1. Preheat the oven to 400°F.

2. Place the mushrooms, onion, garlic, and rosemary on a baking sheet. Pour the olive oil over the vegetables and rosemary, season everything with the salt and pepper, and toss to coat.

3. Roast the vegetables and herbs, stirring occasionally, until tender, about 25 minutes.

4. Remove the pan from the oven and squeeze the garlic cloves from their skins. Discard the skins.

5. Transfer the vegetables to a large pot and add the broth and potatoes. Bring the soup to a boil over medium-high heat. Once it boils, reduce the heat to medium and simmer until the potatoes are tender, about 15 minutes.

6. Remove and discard the rosemary sprigs. Using an immersion blender, blend the soup until it is uniformly creamy.

Tip: Want the soup even creamier? Swap in 2 cups of dairy-free creamer for 2 cups of the veggie broth.

CARAMELIZED BUTTERNUT SQUASH AND APPLE BISQUE WITH BACON-CHEDDAR CROUTONS

Prep Time: 15 minutes **Cook Time:** 1 hour 5 minutes
Nut-Free, Soy-Free / **Serves 4**

I like to serve this comforting autumn bisque in a mug for extra coziness. The bacon croutons add not only a crunch, but also a wonderful smoky saltiness. The apple-sauce gives this soup a delicious sweet-tart flavor. Double the recipe and save leftover soup for later. Store in a resealable container in the refrigerator for up to 5 days or in the freezer for up to 3 months.

1 large butternut squash (about
    2½ pounds), peeled, seeded, and cut into
    2-inch pieces
2 russet potatoes, peeled, cut into
    2-inch pieces
2 medium onions, peeled and halved
3 garlic cloves, peeled
¼ cup olive oil
Salt

Freshly ground black pepper
2 sprigs thyme
1 cup applesauce
8 slices gluten-free baguette or
    4 slices gluten-free bread, cut into
    triangles, toasted
4 slices bacon, chopped and cooked
    until crisp
Dairy-free shredded cheddar, for sprinkling

1. Preheat the oven to 400°F. On two baking sheets, toss the squash, potatoes, onions, and garlic with olive oil to coat. Season the vegetables generously with salt and pepper.

2. Roast the vegetables until caramelized, stirring halfway through the baking time, about 40 minutes. Transfer the roasted vegetables to a soup pot and add enough water to cover by 2 inches. Stir in the thyme and simmer, covered, for 20 minutes. Discard the thyme sprigs.

3. Using an immersion blender, blend the soup until creamy. Add water to reach the desired consistency, and season to taste with salt and pepper. Stir in the applesauce and heat to a simmer.

4. Preheat the broiler. Place 4 ovenproof mugs on a baking sheet and fill each with soup. Top each mug with 2 baguette slices sprinkled with the bacon and cheddar. Broil until the cheese is bubbling, about 2 minutes.

Tip: No gluten-free bread? Just omit it or replace it with toasted gluten-free plain mini waffles.

GRILLED ROMAINE WITH CREAMY CAESAR DRESSING AND CHICKPEA CROUTONS

Prep Time: 10 minutes **Cook Time:** 25 minutes
Nut-Free, Soy-Free / **Serves 4**

The grilled romaine in this salad works nicely with the cool, creamy Caesar dressing. If you don't have the "Grated" Parmesan Cheese (page 111) on hand, swap in some toasted pine nuts or walnuts for flavor and texture. Short on time? Serve the romaine uncooked, or make the dressing ahead of time and store it in the refrigerator for up to 3 days.

1 (15.5-ounce) can chickpeas, rinsed
   and drained
4 tablespoons olive oil, divided, plus more
   for rubbing
¼ teaspoon cayenne pepper
1¼ teaspoons salt, divided
½ teaspoon freshly ground black
   pepper, divided

½ cup mayonnaise
1½ teaspoons Dijon mustard
½ teaspoon Worcestershire sauce
1 garlic clove, chopped
Zest and juice of ½ lemon
4 romaine hearts, halved lengthwise
"Grated" Parmesan Cheese (page 111)

1. Preheat the oven to 400°F.

2. On a rimmed baking sheet, toss the chickpeas with 2 tablespoons olive oil and the cayenne pepper, ½ teaspoon salt, and ¼ teaspoon black pepper. Bake, shaking the pan occasionally, until the chickpeas are golden and crisp, about 20 minutes.

3. Meanwhile, using a food processor or blender, combine the mayonnaise, mustard, Worcestershire sauce, garlic, lemon juice, and remaining olive oil until creamy.

4. Preheat a grill or grill pan to medium-high heat. Rub the romaine hearts with olive oil and season them with the remaining ¾ teaspoon salt and ¼ teaspoon pepper. Grill the romaine hearts for 3 minutes, turning them occasionally, until slightly charred. Place the grilled romaine on a serving platter, drizzle it with the creamy dressing, and top with the "Grated" Parmesan Cheese, lemon zest, and chickpea croutons.

Tip: Want more umami? Add 1 anchovy fillet to the salad dressing ingredients before blending.

QUICK TACO SALAD

Prep Time: 15 minutes **Cook Time:** 10 minutes

Soy-Free, 30 Minutes or Less, One Pot / **Serves 4**

Taco salad is at the top of my family's all-time favorite salads. Need a quick fix? Swap store-bought rotisserie chicken for the ground turkey and replace the Magic Creamy Cilantro Dressing with 2 parts salsa combined with 1 part store-bought dairy-free ranch dressing.

1 tablespoon olive oil

½ pound ground turkey

Taco seasoning

6 cups fresh spinach, chopped

½ cup shredded carrots

1 cup cherry tomatoes, halved

¼ red onion, chopped

1 (15.5-ounce) can black beans, rinsed
   and drained

½ bell pepper, chopped

1 cup Magic Creamy Cilantro Dressing
   (page 116)

¼ cup shredded dairy-free cheddar cheese

1 large avocado, diced

½ cup crumbled tortilla chips

1. Heat the oil in a medium skillet over medium-high heat. Add the ground turkey and break it up with a wooden spoon; season the meat with taco seasoning. Stir and cook until the meat is cooked through, about 8 minutes. Let the meat cool, then add more taco seasoning to taste.

2. Divide the spinach, carrots, tomatoes, onion, beans, bell pepper, cooked turkey, dressing, cheese, avocado, and tortilla chips evenly among 4 serving bowls.

Tip: Layer on more Tex-Mex flavor with cooked corn kernels, fresh or pickled jalapeño pepper, and a squeeze of lime.

Hurry Curry
Page 59

Chapter Five

VEGETABLE MAINS AND SIDES

SOUTHWESTERN STUFFED SWEET POTATOES

Prep Time: 10 minutes **Cook Time:** 20 minutes

Soy-Free, 30 Minutes or Less / **Serves 4**

Rather than accentuating the sweetness of sweet potatoes, this savory veggie side adds spice. You can make this recipe ahead of time and refrigerate it for up to 5 days; it also freezes well. Just wrap each loaded potato in foil, then place them in a resealable freezer bag. To reheat, thaw the stuffed potatoes overnight in the refrigerator and cook them in a 350°F degree oven until warmed through, about 20 minutes.

4 medium sweet potatoes

1 (14.5-ounce) can black beans, rinsed and drained

6 ounces frozen roasted corn

½ cup dairy-free shredded cheddar cheese

Salt

Freshly ground black pepper

1 large avocado, chopped

½ bunch cilantro leaves, chopped

½ cup Creamy Chipotle Sauce (page 117) or store-bought salsa

4 tablespoons roasted pumpkin seeds

1. Pierce the sweet potatoes all over with a fork, then wrap them with paper towels. Microwave the potatoes on high until tender, 5 to 8 minutes. Let the potatoes sit until they are cool enough to handle.

2. Preheat the oven to 425°F and line a baking sheet with parchment paper.

3. Cut each potato in half lengthwise, and carefully scrape the flesh into a large mixing bowl, being careful not to tear the shell and leaving a small rim of potato; place the skins on the prepared baking sheet.

4. Add the black beans, corn, and cheese to the sweet potato flesh, mix well, and season to taste with salt and pepper. Spoon the filling into each potato skin, and bake for 10 minutes.

5. Let the stuffed potatoes cool slightly, then top each with ¼ avocado, 1 tablespoon cilantro, 2 tablespoons Creamy Chipotle Sauce, and 1 tablespoon pumpkin seeds.

VEGETABLE LASAGNA

Prep Time: 15 minutes **Cook Time:** 40 minutes, plus 20 minutes to rest
Serves 8

This flavorful lasagna is packed with mushrooms, onion, and zucchini. I like to use cashew milk for its creaminess, but you can use almond milk or coconut milk instead. If the lasagna edges start to burn during baking, cover them with foil, then remove the foil for the last 5 minutes of cooking.

1 (9-ounce) package gluten-free
  lasagna noodles
Nonstick cooking spray
2 tablespoons olive oil
2 cups sliced mushrooms
1 large white onion, chopped
1 large zucchini, chopped
1 yellow squash, chopped
Salt
Freshly ground black pepper

2 cups dairy-free ricotta cheese or
  Creamy Ricotta (page 112)
4 tablespoons unsweetened cashew milk
2 large eggs
2 teaspoons dried oregano
2 teaspoons dried basil
1 (25-ounce) jar marinara sauce
2 cups shredded dairy-free
  mozzarella cheese

1. Cook the noodles according to the package directions. Coat a 9-by-13-inch baking dish with nonstick cooking spray.

2. Preheat the oven to 375°F. In a medium saucepan, heat the oil over medium-low heat. Add the mushrooms, onion, zucchini, yellow squash, and a pinch each of salt and pepper. Cook, stirring often, until the vegetables are softened, about 10 minutes.

3. In a large bowl, stir together the ricotta cheese, milk, eggs, oregano, and basil.

CONTINUED

4. Spread about one-quarter of the marinara sauce on the bottom of the prepared baking dish. Place one-quarter of the noodles in a single layer over the sauce. Spread the noodles with one-third of the ricotta mixture, then top with one-third of the cooked vegetables. Repeat the layers two more times, starting with tomato sauce, then noodles, ricotta mixture, and vegetables. Cover with the fourth layer of noodles and top with the remaining tomato sauce and the shredded mozzarella.

5. Bake until the cheese is bubbling and the center is hot, about 40 minutes. Let the lasagna rest for 20 minutes before serving.

Tip: You can assemble the lasagna in the morning and refrigerate it until you're ready to bake. Just add 15 minutes to the cooking time.

BUTTERNUT SQUASH MAC AND CHEESE

Prep Time: 15 minutes **Cook Time:** 55 minutes
Soy-Free, Vegan / **Serves 6**

This comforting dish makes the perfect meal in the winter when butternut squash is in season. Want to speed up the recipe? Cook and puree the squash ahead of time. Then, all you need to do is stir the squash into the noodles.

1 medium butternut squash, peeled, seeded, and cut into 1-inch pieces

1 tablespoon olive oil

1 small onion

2 garlic cloves

1 cup cashew milk

¼ cup nutritional yeast

2 tablespoons dairy-free unsalted butter

1 tablespoon Dijon mustard

¾ teaspoon salt

¼ teaspoon freshly ground black pepper

1 (16-ounce) package gluten-free elbow macaroni

1. Preheat the oven to 400°F and line a baking sheet with parchment paper. Place the squash on the baking sheet and drizzle it with the oil; toss to coat and then drizzle the squash with a little water. Wrap the onion and garlic cloves in a piece of foil and place them on the baking sheet. Roast until the squash is tender, about 45 minutes; remove the pan from the oven and let the roasted vegetables cool slightly.

2. In a blender, combine the roasted squash, onion, and garlic with the milk, nutritional yeast, butter, mustard, salt, and pepper. Puree until the mixture is smooth and creamy.

3. Meanwhile, cook the macaroni in a pot of salted boiling water according to the package directions; drain the macaroni and return it to the pot.

4. Pour the squash sauce over the macaroni and toss to coat; season with salt and pepper to taste, then serve.

Tip: No elbow macaroni in your pantry? Swap in any gluten-free short pasta, like penne, rotini, or farfalle.

QUICK PAD THAI

Prep Time: 10 minutes, plus 30 minutes to soak **Cook Time:** 10 minutes
Serves 4

I always stock up on rice noodles because they cook fast, soak up sauce well, and have the perfect texture for a noodle bowl like this pad Thai. Make this recipe your own—go ahead and swap in whatever veggies you have on hand.

1 (14-ounce) package rice noodles

3 tablespoons avocado oil

1 (14-ounce) package firm tofu, cut into 1-inch pieces

3 garlic cloves, finely chopped

1 teaspoon sesame oil

¼ cup coconut aminos or gluten-free tamari

3 tablespoons pure maple syrup

Juice of 1 lime

1 teaspoon white vinegar

¼ cup water

2 cups bean sprouts

½ cup shredded carrot

¼ cup chopped scallions (green parts only)

Crushed peanuts, for serving

Chopped fresh chives, for topping (optional)

Chopped fresh cilantro, for topping (optional)

Lime wedges, for topping

1. In a large bowl of warm water, soak the noodles for at least 30 minutes but no longer than 1 hour.

2. Heat the oil in a large nonstick pan over medium-high heat. Add the tofu and cook, turning, until golden all over, about 3 minutes. Using a spatula, move the tofu to the side of the pan.

3. Reduce the heat to medium and add the garlic, sesame oil, coconut aminos, maple syrup, lime juice, and vinegar to the pan; stir for 30 seconds. Drain the soaked noodles and add them to the sauce; toss to coat. Stir in ¼ cup water and cook the noodles until they are tender and the water has evaporated, about 3 minutes.

4. Remove the pan from the heat and add the bean sprouts, carrots, and scallions; toss the vegetables with the noodle mixture.

5. Top each serving with crushed peanuts, chopped chives and cilantro (if using), and a lime wedge.

HURRY CURRY

Prep Time: 10 minutes **Cook Time:** 35 minutes
Soy-Free, Vegan, One Pot / **Serves 6**

This curry cooks up fast any day of the week. Want to make it a meal?
Stir in cubed firm tofu or shredded store-bought rotisserie chicken along with
the spinach.

1 tablespoon coconut oil	2 cups chopped butternut squash
1 yellow onion, chopped	1 cup chopped broccoli
2 tablespoons grated fresh ginger	1 cup chopped red bell pepper
2 garlic cloves, finely chopped	1 cup chopped eggplant
3 tablespoons curry powder	1 (4-ounce) can coconut cream
1 tablespoon ground cumin	⅓ cup vegetable broth
1 tablespoon tomato paste	4 cups fresh spinach

1. Heat the coconut oil in a large pot over medium-high heat. Add the onion, ginger, and garlic and cook until softened, about 3 minutes. Stir in the curry powder, cumin, and tomato paste; cook until fragrant, about 1 minute. Stir in the squash, broccoli, bell pepper, eggplant, coconut cream, and vegetable broth. Reduce the heat to low and simmer until thickened, about 30 minutes.

2. Remove the pot from the heat, stir in the spinach, cover the pot, and cook until the spinach wilts, about 3 minutes.

Tip: Serve this curry over cooked rice, quinoa, boiled potatoes, or even gluten-free noodles.

EASY MARGHERITA PIZZA

Prep Time: 15 minutes **Cook Time:** 25 minutes

Soy-Free, Vegan / **Serves 8**

A big slice of authentic-tasting pizza? Yes, please. You'll get this pizza on the table in less time than ordering takeout. If you can't find a dairy-free mozzarella ball, use shredded mozzarella instead.

For the pizza dough

3 cups Gluten-Free All-Purpose Flour
    (page 4) or store-bought blend, plus more
    for dusting
2¼ teaspoons (1 packet) active dry yeast

¼ teaspoon salt
1 cup warm water (120°F to 130°F)
2 tablespoons olive oil

For the pizza

Nonstick cooking spray
¼ cup tomato paste
½ teaspoon garlic powder
Salt

Freshly ground black pepper
Dairy-free mozzarella ball, thinly sliced
6 fresh basil leaves

1. **To make the pizza dough:** Preheat the oven to 375°F. In a medium bowl, whisk together the flour, yeast, and salt. Add the water and oil; stir to combine. Place the dough on a flour-dusted surface and knead until smooth and elastic, about 8 minutes. Divide the dough into two balls, and using a rolling pin, roll them out to form two 9-inch pizza crusts.

2. **To make the pizza:** Working with one dough round at a time, grease a pizza pan or baking sheet with cooking spray and place a pizza crust on top. Spread it with half of the tomato paste, leaving a ½-inch border, then sprinkle it with garlic powder, salt, and pepper to taste. Top with half of the cheese slices. Repeat with the remaining pizza crust and toppings. Bake until the crusts are golden and the cheese is melted, about 25 minutes. To serve, top each pizza with half of the basil.

GIARDINIERA POTATO SALAD

Prep Time: 15 minutes **Cook Time:** 10 minutes, plus 1 hour to chill
Nut-Free, Soy-Free, Vegan / **Serves 4**

Over the years, I've come up with easy, picnic-friendly foods, including this Italian-inspired potato salad. If you're not familiar with giardiniera—which literally means "woman gardener" in Italian—it's a classic relish of pickled vegetables packed in vinegar, herbs, and spices, made to preserve the summer harvest. Once the warm potatoes are tossed with the giardiniera and Dijon vinaigrette, it's hard to keep from eating the whole bowl.

2 pounds medium red potatoes, cut into 1-inch pieces

½ cup giardiniera

2 teaspoons Dijon mustard

2 tablespoons apple cider vinegar

2 tablespoons red onion, finely chopped

½ cup fresh basil leaves, chopped

¼ cup olive oil

¾ teaspoon salt

⅛ teaspoon freshly ground black pepper

1. In a large pot of salted water, bring the potatoes to a boil over medium heat. Reduce the heat and simmer until fork tender, about 10 minutes. Drain the potatoes and place them in a large bowl with the giardiniera.

2. In a small bowl, whisk together the mustard, vinegar, onion, and basil. Whisking continuously, add the olive oil in a slow, steady stream until combined. Pour over the potatoes and toss gently. Season with the salt and pepper. Refrigerate the salad until it is thoroughly chilled, about 1 hour.

Tip: Add more texture and flavor by stirring in chopped marinated charred artichoke hearts and pitted mixed olives.

Tip: Use the Dijon vinaigrette and giardiniera from this recipe instead of the classic mayo for a flavor-packed take on tuna salad.

GREEN BEAN–MUSHROOM CASSEROLE WITH PANKO-STYLE FRIED ONION RINGS

Prep Time: 20 minutes **Cook Time:** 40 minutes
Soy-Free, Vegan / **Serves 8**

I was never a big fan of casseroles, especially this traditional Thanksgiving green bean–mushroom kind. I knew I wanted to ultimately prove myself wrong, and in re-creating this side dish to be gluten-free and dairy-free, I realized the secret was all in the crispy fried onions on top.

For the onion rings

Vegetable oil, for frying
¼ cup Gluten-Free All-Purpose Flour
(page 4) or store-bought blend

¼ cup crushed gluten-free rice cereal
1 teaspoon salt
1 large onion, cut into thin rings

For the casserole

2 tablespoons olive oil
8 ounces mushrooms, sliced
Salt
Freshly ground black pepper
2 tablespoons Gluten-Free All-Purpose
Flour (page 4) or store-bought blend

¾ cup vegetable broth
¾ cup dairy-free creamer
1 pound green beans, trimmed and
blanched
½ teaspoon chili powder

To make the onion rings:

1. Preheat the oven to 375°F and grease an 8-by-8-inch baking dish.

2. In a large pot, pour in enough oil to reach the depth of about 1 inch, then heat it over medium-high heat until the oil registers 350°F on a deep-frying thermometer. Line a plate with paper towels.

3. In a small bowl, whisk together the flour, rice cereal, and salt.

4. Add the sliced onion rings to the flour mixture and toss to coat them evenly. Working in batches, fry the onion rings in the oil until golden brown and lightly crisped, 3 to 5 minutes. Transfer the fried onions to the prepared paper towels to drain.

To make the green beans:

5. In a large skillet, heat the olive oil over medium-high heat. Add the mushrooms and cook, stirring occasionally, until the oil has evaporated.

6. Season the mushrooms with salt and pepper, then sprinkle the flour over them and cook, stirring, for 1 minute.

7. Stir in the broth and creamer, bring to a simmer, and cook until thickened, about 4 minutes. Stir in the green beans and season with the chili powder and salt and pepper to taste. Transfer the mixture to the prepared baking dish and top with the fried onion rings. Bake until golden and bubbling, 25 to 30 minutes.

Fish Tacos with
Pineapple-Mango Salsa
Page 67

Chapter Six

FISH AND SEAFOOD

RED CURRY SALMON AND VEGETABLE PACKETS

Prep Time: 10 minutes **Cook Time:** 10 minutes
Soy-Free, 30 Minutes or Less / **Serves 4**

This recipe is a take on Thai curry soup, combining all the same fragrant flavors in easy foil packets that you can cook in the oven or, on hot summer days, on your grill. For less heat, replace the red curry paste with a milder yellow or green curry paste.

4 (4-ounce) salmon fillets

4 Thai chiles (optional)

2 cups snow peas

1 medium red onion, sliced

1 bell pepper, stem, ribs, and seeds removed, sliced lengthwise

1 tablespoon Thai red curry paste

1 tablespoon fish sauce

Juice of 1 lime

2 garlic cloves, grated

½-inch piece fresh ginger, peeled and grated (about 2 teaspoons)

¼ cup full-fat coconut milk

2 tablespoons chopped fresh basil

2 tablespoons chopped fresh cilantro

1. Preheat the oven to 375°F. Place 4 large sheets of foil on a clean surface and position 1 salmon fillet in the center of each. Top each fillet with 1 chile, ½ cup snow peas, and a quarter of the red onion and bell pepper slices.

2. In a small bowl, whisk together the curry paste, fish sauce, lime juice, garlic, ginger, and coconut milk. Drizzle the sauce over the salmon and vegetables. Bring the short ends of the foil together and fold to seal completely; bake until cooked through, about 12 minutes. Remove the packets from the oven, carefully open them, and top the cooked fish with the chopped basil and cilantro.

Tip: The sealed foil packets will keep in the refrigerator for up to 3 days.

FISH TACOS WITH PINEAPPLE-MANGO SALSA

Prep Time: 5 minutes, plus 30 minutes to marinate **Cook Time:** 5 minutes
Nut-Free, Soy-Free / **Serves 4**

Summer calls for easy, oven-free dinners packed with light, refreshing flavors—the definition of these tacos made with flaky mahi-mahi and refreshing pineapple-mango salsa. The doubled-up corn tortillas prevent the tacos from collapsing.

For the salsa

1 cup chopped mango

1 cup chopped pineapple

½ cup finely chopped red onion

1 jalapeño pepper, seeded and
   finely chopped

¼ cup chopped fresh cilantro

Juice of 1 lime

Pinch of salt

For the tacos

¼ cup olive oil

¼ cup chopped fresh cilantro

Juice of 1 lime

1 jalapeño pepper, seeded and
   finely chopped

1 pound mahi-mahi fillets

16 corn tortillas, warmed

To make the salsa:

1. In a small bowl, stir together the mango, pineapple, onion, jalapeño pepper, cilantro, lime juice, and salt; cover and refrigerate.

CONTINUED

To make the tacos:

2. In a small bowl, whisk together the oil, cilantro, lime juice, and jalapeño.

3. Place the fish in a medium bowl. Pour the oil mixture over the fish, cover the bowl, and let the fish marinate in the refrigerator for about 30 minutes.

4. Heat a nonstick skillet over medium-high heat. Remove the fish from the marinade and cook on one side for 4 minutes; flip and cook for 1 minute more. Transfer the fish to a plate and flake it into chunks with a fork. Divide the fish and salsa among warmed doubled-up tortillas.

. . . .

Tip: To warm the tortillas, wrap them in foil and place them in a 350°F oven until heated through, 10 to 15 minutes, or microwave the stack of tortillas on high for 30 seconds.

SHRIMP FETTUCCINE ALFREDO

Prep Time: 10 minutes **Cook Time:** 20 minutes

Soy-Free, 30 Minutes or Less / **Serves 4**

While traditional Italians would never add Parmesan to a fish dish, the dairy-free Parmesan adds a nutty, umami layer of flavor that people love. To give this pasta dish a bit of fresh flavor, sometimes I sprinkle chopped parsley or lemon zest on top just before serving. If you prefer to make your sauce extra creamy, use the Easy Nut or Seed Milk recipe (page 107) and reduce the water from 4 cups to 2 cups.

16 large shrimp, peeled, deveined, and
   tails removed
Salt
Freshly ground black pepper
8 tablespoons dairy-free butter, divided

1½ cups dairy-free unsweetened creamer
1 cup "Grated" Parmesan (page 111), divided
Pinch ground nutmeg
1 (12-ounce) box gluten-free fettuccine

1. Pat the shrimp dry with paper towels, then season with salt and pepper.

2. Heat 2 tablespoons of butter in a large saucepan over medium heat until melted. Increase the heat to medium-high and add the shrimp in a single layer. Cook until cooked through and golden, turning once, about 4 minutes total. Transfer the cooked shrimp to a plate.

3. Reduce the heat to medium and add the remaining 6 tablespoons butter, scraping up any browned bits from the bottom of the pan with a wooden spoon. Whisk in the creamer and bring the mixture to a boil. Reduce the heat to low and simmer for 5 minutes or until slightly reduced. Whisk in ½ cup Parmesan until the sauce is smooth, and season with salt, pepper, and nutmeg.

4. Bring a large pot of salted water to a boil. Add the pasta and cook until al dente, about 10 minutes, then drain.

5. To serve, add the cooked pasta and shrimp to the cream sauce, toss to coat, and top with the remaining ½ cup Parmesan.

Tip: To make this a vegetarian meal, omit the shrimp or swap in sauteed ribbons of zucchini instead.

CAULIFLOWER, BROCCOLI, AND SHRIMP TART

Prep Time: 20 minutes **Cook Time:** 45 minutes
Soy-Free / **Serves 8**

I love the versatility of tarts, and they're perfect for brunch or dinner served with a salad alongside. To make this dish vegan, skip the shrimp and add ½ cup more cauliflower.

For the crust

1 cup Gluten-Free All-Purpose Flour (page 4) or store-bought blend, plus more for dusting
¼ cup almond meal
1 teaspoon dried dill

½ teaspoon dried tarragon
¼ teaspoon salt
6 tablespoons cold water
4 tablespoons dairy-free butter
Nonstick cooking spray

For the filling

4 tablespoons dairy-free butter
¾ cup finely chopped yellow onion
½ cup finely chopped cauliflower florets
½ cup finely chopped broccoli florets
1 tablespoon Gluten-Free All-Purpose Flour (page 4) or store-bought blend
½ cup vegetable broth

1⅓ cups shredded dairy-free mozzarella cheese, divided
1 (5-ounce) can baby shrimp, drained
Salt
Freshly ground black pepper
Paprika, for sprinkling

To make the crust:

1. In a medium bowl, stir together the flour, almond meal, dill, tarragon, salt, and water. With a pastry blender or two knives, cut in the butter until coarse crumbs form. Using your hands or a silicone spatula, form the mixture into a dough.

2. Preheat the oven to 375°F and coat a 9-inch round tart pan with nonstick cooking spray. On a lightly floured piece of parchment paper, roll the dough into a 10-inch round. Flip the parchment paper over the tart pan, reserving the paper, and press the dough round to evenly cover the bottom and sides of the pan.

3. Using a fork, prick the bottom of the dough a few times, then cover the dough with the reserved parchment paper; bake for 15 minutes. Remove the parchment paper and bake until lightly browned, about 5 minutes more.

To make the filling:

4. In a large skillet, melt the butter over medium-high heat. Add the onion, cauliflower, and broccoli; cook, stirring, until fork-tender, about 5 minutes. Add the flour and cook, stirring, for 1 minute. Stir in the broth and bring to a boil; remove from the heat. Add 1 cup of the mozzarella and the shrimp; stir until the cheese is melted, then season with salt and pepper.

5. Spoon the filling into the tart shell. Sprinkle with the remaining ⅓ cup mozzarella and bake until hot and bubbling, about 10 minutes. Sprinkle with paprika and let stand for at least 5 minutes before cutting into 8 wedges.

Tip: Prefer fresh shrimp? Just use 5 ounces of cooked baby shrimp or chopped small shrimp in place of the canned.

CRISPY FISH NUGGETS WITH LEMON TARTAR SAUCE

Prep Time: 15 minutes **Cook Time:** 20 minutes
Nut-Free, Soy-Free / **Serves 4**

No more frozen fish sticks! Instead, make these gluten-free beer-battered fish nuggets and lemony tartar sauce for dipping. I like to add gluten-free beer to the batter, which makes the nuggets light and airy, but seltzer can also be used.

1 cup Gluten-Free All-Purpose Flour
   (page 4) or store-bought blend, plus more
   for dredging
1½ cups finely crushed gluten-free
   corn flakes
1½ teaspoons baking powder
2 tablespoons paprika
1 teaspoon garlic powder
1½ teaspoons salt
Freshly ground black pepper

1½ cups cold gluten-free light beer
   or seltzer
2 egg whites, beaten
¾ cup mayonnaise
Zest and juice of 1 lemon, plus lemon
   wedges for serving
3 tablespoons Dijon mustard
3 tablespoons capers packed in salt, rinsed
2 pounds halibut or cod fillets, cut into
   ½-inch-wide strips and patted dry
Vegetable oil, for frying

1. In a food processor, combine the flour, corn flakes, baking powder, paprika, garlic powder, salt, and pepper to taste. Add the beer and egg whites, and process until smooth. Cover and refrigerate for 15 minutes.

2. To make the tartar sauce: In a small bowl, stir together the mayonnaise, lemon zest and juice, mustard, and capers. Season the sauce with salt and pepper and refrigerate it.

3. Fill a large pot with enough oil to reach a depth of 1 inch, and heat it over medium-high heat until it registers 350°F on a deep-frying thermometer.

4. Working in batches, lightly dredge the fish strips in flour, then coat them with the batter. Fry, turning once, until golden brown, about 4 minutes total. Remove the fried nuggets with a slotted spoon and drain them on paper towels. Season the fish with salt and serve with the tartar sauce.

SALMON SCAMPI

Prep Time: 15 minutes **Cook Time:** 20 minutes
Soy-Free / **Serves 6**

My family loves salmon—grilled for kebabs, flaked for tacos, or delicately cooked *en papillote*. One night, as I was staring at a plank of salmon I picked up from my local fishmonger, I decided to take the flavors of traditional shrimp scampi and make a hearty main dish using salmon instead. Roasting a whole side of salmon makes for a bold dinner centerpiece. Go ahead and use gluten-free breadcrumbs in place of the rice cereal if you like.

¾ cup finely crushed gluten-free rice cereal

¼ cup pine nuts, finely chopped

4 garlic cloves, finely chopped

2 tablespoons fresh parsley, finely chopped

2 tablespoons olive oil

2 tablespoons vermouth

½ teaspoon red pepper flakes

1 teaspoon salt

Freshly ground black pepper

2½ pounds whole side salmon, skin on

Lemon wedges, for serving

1. Preheat the oven to 400°F and line a baking sheet with parchment paper.

2. In a small bowl, stir together the cereal, pine nuts, garlic, parsley, oil, vermouth, red pepper flakes, and salt.

3. Place the salmon skin-side down on the prepared baking sheet. Season it generously with salt and pepper. Cover the fish completely with the cereal mixture and bake until cooked through, about 20 minutes. Serve with lemon wedges.

Tip: No vermouth? Swap in an equal amount of white wine, vegetable broth, or even water.

MUSSELS MARINARA WITH GARLIC BREAD DIPPERS

Prep Time: 10 minutes **Cook Time:** 15 minutes
Nut-Free, Soy-Free, 30 Minutes or Less / **Serves 4**

My Italian grandfather used to cook this dish for my brother and me when we visited him for summers in Italy. We'd tear through a loaf of crusty Italian bread to soak up all the briny juices. Here, I toast a baguette and slather it generously with melted garlic butter made with garlic powder. I don't use fresh garlic in order to avoid any burning.

For the mussels

6 tablespoons olive oil

2 garlic cloves, smashed

½ pound cherry tomatoes, halved

½ cup dry white wine

2 pounds mussels, cleaned and debearded

¼ cup chopped fresh mint

¼ cup chopped fresh basil

For the garlic bread dippers

1 store-bought gluten-free baguette, halved lengthwise

½ cup dairy-free unsalted butter, melted

1½ teaspoons garlic powder

1 teaspoon salt

To make the mussels:

1. In a large saucepan, heat the olive oil over medium-high heat until hot but not smoking. Add the garlic and cook until golden, about 1 minute.

2. Add the tomatoes and cover the pot. Let the tomatoes soften, about 5 minutes.

3. Add the wine and cook, uncovered, until the alcohol evaporates, about 3 minutes.

4. Add the mussels, mint, and basil, shaking the pot gently.

5. Cover the pot and let the mussels cook until they open, about 3 minutes. Discard any mussels that do not open. Remove the saucepan from the heat.

To make the garlic bread:

6. Preheat the oven to 450°F. Place the baguette halves cut-side up on a parchment-lined baking sheet.

7. In a small bowl, stir together the butter, garlic powder, and salt.

8. Brush the butter mixture onto the baguette halves.

9. Cut the baguette halves crosswise into 1-inch-thick slices, being careful not to cut through the bottom crust.

10. Bake the baguette until golden, about 10 minutes.

....

Tip: To add a little kick, stir 1 teaspoon of red pepper flakes into the garlic butter.

SEARED SCALLOPS WITH HORSERADISH SAUCE

Prep Time: 10 minutes **Cook Time:** 3 minutes
Nut-Free, Soy-Free, 30 Minutes or Less / **Serves 4**

After ordering this dish more times than I can remember, I decided it was time for me to figure out how to make it in my own kitchen. Turns out, it was way easier than I thought and tastier than I remembered. The best part? The salty crust and buttery texture. This quick and easy horseradish sauce gives the scallops a nice tang with a hint of heat. For best results, remove the small side muscle in each scallop before searing. While that part of the scallop is edible, it takes longer to cook than the rest of the scallop, which means it will still be tough and chewy when you take the scallops out of the skillet.

For the sauce

½ cup mayonnaise

1 (6-ounce) jar prepared horseradish, drained

2 teaspoons Dijon mustard

1 teaspoon apple cider vinegar

1 tablespoon sugar

½ teaspoon salt

⅛ teaspoon freshly ground black pepper

For the scallops

Salt

Freshly ground black pepper

1 pound dry-packed sea scallops, rinsed
   and patted dry

2 teaspoons dairy-free unsalted butter

2 teaspoons olive oil

To make the sauce:

1. In a small bowl, combine the mayonnaise, horseradish, mustard, vinegar, and sugar until blended.

2. Season the sauce with salt and pepper.

To make the scallops:

3. Salt and pepper the scallops.

4. Heat the butter and oil in a 12-inch nonstick skillet over high heat until just smoking. Add the scallops, making sure they aren't touching. Cook, turning once, until a golden crust forms, 3 minutes total. Serve with the sauce.

Tip: Skip the sauce and top the seared scallops with a squeeze of lemon and finely chopped parsley instead.

SWEET CHILI SNAPPER

Prep Time: 15 minutes **Cook Time:** 15 minutes
Nut-Free, Soy-Free, 30 Minutes or Less / **Serves 4**

This recipe is packed with sweet-and-sour flavors from Thai sweet red chili sauce and lime juice. For added crunch, I top the fish with gluten-free crushed rice cereal drizzled with olive oil before roasting.

Grated zest of 1 lime

3 tablespoons lime juice, divided

5½ tablespoons store-bought gluten-free Thai sweet red chili sauce, divided

2 tablespoons chopped fresh cilantro

¼ cup plus 2 tablespoons olive oil, divided, plus more for greasing and drizzling

¼ teaspoon salt

1 seedless cucumber, peeled and cut into matchsticks

½ red onion, cut into matchsticks

1 red bell pepper, seeded and cut into matchsticks

2 jalapeño peppers, seeded and cut into matchsticks

4 (6-ounce) red snapper fillets, patted dry

½ cup finely crushed gluten-free rice cereal

1. In a medium bowl, whisk together the lime zest, 2 tablespoons lime juice, 1½ tablespoons chili sauce, and cilantro. Whisking continuously, add ¼ cup oil in a slow, steady stream until combined. Season with about ¼ teaspoon salt. Add the cucumber, onion, bell pepper, and jalapeños. Toss to coat, then cover and refrigerate.

2. Preheat the oven to 425°F and line a baking sheet with parchment paper. In a small bowl, stir together the remaining ¼ cup chili sauce and 1 tablespoon lime juice.

3. Place the fish, skin-side down, on the prepared baking sheet. Season the fillets generously with salt and brush them with the chili-lime sauce. Sprinkle the fish with the cereal and drizzle generously with oil.

4. Roast until cooked through, about 12 minutes. To serve, top with the veggie slaw.

Tip: Swap the red snapper for a favorite fish or seafood like salmon, tuna, halibut, shrimp, or scallops.

Healthy Summer Spaghetti
Page 82

Chapter Seven

MEAT AND POULTRY

HEALTHY SUMMER SPAGHETTI

Prep Time: 15 minutes **Cook Time:** 30 minutes
Nut-Free, Soy-Free / **Serves 6**

This mouthwatering pasta dish is a great way to use a bumper crop of fresh zucchini, yellow squash, and juicy tomatoes in the summer. For more flavor, add grilled eggplant and sliced black olives.

2 large zucchinis, ends removed

2 yellow squash, ends removed

Salt

Nonstick cooking spray

1 white onion, cut into ½-inch rings

1½ tablespoons olive oil

1 (16-ounce) package gluten-free spaghetti

4 tomatoes

1 (32-ounce) jar marinara sauce

2 cooked chicken breasts, cut into
    1-inch pieces

¼ cup chopped fresh basil

1. Cut the zucchini and yellow squash lengthwise in half, then cut each in half again so you have 4 long, thin strips. Sprinkle the pieces with salt.

2. Coat the grates of a grill or grill pan with nonstick cooking spray and preheat to high.

3. Using a paper towel, blot the zucchini and squash to remove any excess water; place the squash and onion in a large bowl and toss with the oil.

4. Reduce the grill temperature to medium-high. Arrange the vegetables on the grates and cook, turning once, until slightly charred and softened, about 20 minutes total; place on a cutting board.

5. In a large pot, cook the pasta according to the package directions.

6. Meanwhile, chop the zucchini, yellow squash, onion, and tomatoes.

7. Drain the pasta and return it to the pot. Add the marinara sauce, chicken, grilled vegetables, and tomatoes; toss to coat. Cook over low heat, stirring, for 2 minutes to heat through. To serve, top with the basil.

Tip: Instead of grilling, roast the vegetables. Place them on a parchment-lined baking sheet and roast, turning once, in a 425°F oven until golden and softened, about 20 minutes total.

SHEET PAN ITALIAN CHICKEN WITH BRUSSELS SPROUTS

Prep Time: 10 minutes **Cook Time:** 30 minutes

Nut-Free, Soy-Free, 5 Ingredient / **Serves 6**

Crispy bacon, caramelized Brussels sprouts, and chicken breasts all drizzled with balsamic vinegar syrup? Yes, please. Plus, everything is cooked on one baking sheet. Translation? Minimal cleanup.

1½ pounds Brussels sprouts, trimmed
  and halved

4 tablespoons olive oil, divided

4 ounces peppered bacon, cut into
  ¼-inch pieces

Salt

Freshly ground black pepper

4 chicken breasts, about 1½ pounds

Italian seasoning

2 tablespoons balsamic vinegar

1. Preheat the oven to 400°F and line a baking sheet with parchment paper.

2. Place the Brussels sprouts on the prepared baking sheet and drizzle them with 3 tablespoons oil. Add the bacon and season all with salt and pepper; toss to coat and spread evenly in a single layer, making room in the center for the chicken breast pieces. Brush the chicken breasts with the remaining 1 tablespoon oil and season them all over with Italian seasoning, salt, and pepper. Roast, tossing occasionally, until golden and softened, about 25 minutes.

3. Pour the vinegar into a small oven-proof bowl. In the last 5 minutes of cooking, place the bowl on a corner of the baking sheet. Remove the pan from the oven, drizzle the Brussels sprouts and chicken with the reduced vinegar, and toss all to coat; let cool for about 5 minutes before serving.

....

Tip: Not a Brussels sprout fan? Swap in cubed sweet potatoes, winter squash, broccoli, or asparagus.

MEXICAN-STYLE STUFFED BELL PEPPERS

Prep Time: 10 minutes **Cook Time:** 35 minutes
Nut-Free, Soy-Free, 5 Ingredient / **Serves 6**

When you eat these cheesy stuffed peppers, you'll think you're eating tacos—without the tortilla. Although I use Tex-Mex Style Queso (page 118) in this recipe, you could use Magic Creamy Cilantro Dressing (page 116) instead. Leftovers can be easily turned into a satisfying taco salad; just add your favorite greens along with more queso or salsa.

6 large red bell peppers, tops, ribs, and
   seeds removed
Olive oil, for brushing
1 pound ground beef
1 tablespoon taco seasoning, or to taste

1 (14.5-ounce) can black beans, rinsed
   and drained
¾ cup Tex-Mex Style Queso (page 118) or
   store-bought salsa, divided

1. Preheat the oven to 350°F. Place the peppers upright in a baking dish. Brush each pepper with oil and bake until softened, about 15 minutes.

2. Meanwhile, in a medium skillet, cook the beef, breaking it up with a wooden spoon. Sprinkle taco seasoning over the beef and cook it over medium heat until cooked through, about 8 minutes.

3. Stir in the black beans and ½ cup of the Tex-Mex Style Queso into the beef. Using a spoon, fill each pepper with the beef mixture, drizzle the peppers with more queso, and bake until golden brown, about 20 minutes.

Tip: The cooked peppers can be refrigerated for up to 3 days. To reheat them, cover with foil and cook in a 350°F oven for 20 minutes.

CHICKEN CACCIATORE

Prep Time: 10 minutes **Cook Time:** 30 minutes
Nut-Free, Soy-Free / **Serves 4**

You can serve this classic "hunter-style" chicken—a dish traditionally prepared with tomato, peppers, and wine—as is or serve it over cooked gluten-free pasta or spaghetti squash, with a salad alongside. Prefer not to cook with wine? Swap in ¼ cup more of the chicken broth.

⅓ cup Gluten-Free All-Purpose Flour
   (page 4) or store-bought blend
1½ tablespoons Italian seasoning, divided
½ teaspoon salt
½ teaspoon freshly ground black pepper
4 (6-ounce) boneless, skinless chicken
   breasts, pounded about ¼-inch thick
¼ cup olive oil
1½ cups sliced mushrooms

1 green bell pepper, stemmed, seeded,
   and chopped
1 red bell pepper, stemmed, seeded,
   and chopped
1 garlic clove, finely chopped
2 cups canned tomato sauce
½ cup chicken broth
¼ cup dry white wine
1 tablespoon chopped fresh parsley

1. Put the flour, 1 tablespoon of Italian seasoning, and the salt and pepper in a large resealable bag. Add the chicken and seal the bag; shake the bag to coat the chicken well.

2. In a large skillet, heat the oil over medium-high heat. Add the chicken and cook, turning once, until browned, about 4 minutes total. Remove the chicken to a plate.

3. Into the same skillet, put the mushrooms, bell peppers, and garlic. Cook over medium-high heat until softened, about 5 minutes. Add the remaining ½ tablespoon Italian seasoning, tomato sauce, broth, and wine. Bring to a boil and cook for 5 minutes, then reduce the heat to low.

4. Return the chicken to the pan, cover, and simmer for 10 minutes. Uncover and cook until the liquid begins to thicken and the chicken is cooked through, about 5 minutes. To serve, top with the parsley.

SHEET PAN PARMESAN CHICKEN WITH GREEN BEANS

Prep Time: 10 minutes **Cook Time:** 30 minutes

Soy-Free / **Serves 4**

This knockoff recipe will satisfy your cravings for dining out at restaurants. Check all store-bought ingredients, like marinara sauce and Italian seasoning, to make sure they're gluten-free.

Nonstick cooking spray

1 cup cornmeal

¼ cup Italian seasoning

¼ cup "Grated" Parmesan Cheese
  (page 111)

¼ teaspoon salt

4 boneless, skinless chicken breasts

4 cups cut green beans

2 teaspoons olive oil

1 cup marinara sauce

½ cup shredded Sliceable Tangy Mozzarella
  (page 113)

1. Preheat the oven to 400°F and line a baking sheet with foil; lightly coat the foil with cooking spray.

2. In a small bowl, whisk together the cornmeal, Italian seasoning, Parmesan, and salt; coat the chicken with the seasoned meal. Place the coated breasts on half of the prepared baking sheet. Place the green beans on the other half and drizzle them with olive oil. Bake for 20 minutes, then reduce the temperature to 350°F.

3. Spoon the marinara sauce over the chicken and sprinkle it with the mozzarella. Bake until the chicken is cooked through, 10 to 15 minutes more.

Tip: Swap the green beans for another classic restaurant veggie side dish, broccoli.

"FRIED" CHICKEN CUTLETS

Prep Time: 10 minutes **Cook Time:** 20 minutes
Nut-Free, Soy-Free, 5 Ingredient, 30 Minutes or Less / **Serves 4**

This "fried" chicken is healthier—and faster—than traditional cutlets because it's baked, not fried. You can double the recipe and freeze the leftovers in a resealable freezer bag for up to 3 months.

3 tablespoons olive oil, divided

2 large eggs

1¼ cups Gluten-Free All-Purpose Flour (page 4) or store-bought blend

1 tablespoon lemon-pepper seasoning

1 teaspoon paprika

1 teaspoon salt

4 (6-ounce) boneless, skinless chicken breasts, sliced in half lengthwise and pounded thin

1. Preheat the oven to 400°F and brush a baking sheet with 1½ tablespoons of oil.

2. In a small bowl, whisk the eggs. In a baking dish, stir together the flour, lemon-pepper seasoning, paprika, and salt.

3. Working with 1 piece of chicken at a time, coat each with the flour mixture, then the egg, and then the flour mixture again; place the breaded cutlets on the prepared baking sheet. Drizzle the chicken with the remaining 1½ tablespoons oil. Bake until the chicken is cooked through, about 20 minutes.

Tip: Want to make this recipe grain-free? Replace the flour with almond meal.

SLOW COOKER BUFFALO CHICKEN "CHEESE" DIP

Prep Time: 10 minutes **Cook Time:** 2 hours
Soy-Free / **Serves 10 to 12**

This extra-cheesy, spicy buffalo dip will be a fan favorite at your next get-together. The best part? The recipe requires minimal prep and your slow cooker does all the heavy lifting. Serve the dip with raw veggies like cauliflower florets, carrot sticks, and celery sticks or with thick tortilla chips. Store any leftovers in the refrigerator for up to 5 days.

½ cup dairy-free cream cheese

½ cup dairy-free ranch dressing

1 teaspoon garlic powder

1 teaspoon onion powder

¼ cup plain, unsweetened dairy-free yogurt

¼ cup chicken broth, plus more for thinning

½ cup shredded dairy-free cheddar cheese

1 tablespoon nutritional yeast

¼ cup Frank's RedHot Buffalo Wings Sauce, plus more to taste

1 pound boneless, skinless chicken breasts

1. In a mixing bowl, stir together the cream cheese, ranch dressing, garlic powder, onion powder, yogurt, broth, cheddar, nutritional yeast, and hot sauce.

2. Put the chicken breasts in a slow cooker and top them with the cream cheese mixture; stir to coat. Cook on low for 2 hours or on high for 1 hour. Check halfway through cooking and add more broth, if necessary, to thin.

3. Transfer the chicken to a cutting board and shred it with 2 forks; return the shredded chicken to the slow cooker and stir to combine. Season the dip with more hot sauce to taste, and serve hot.

Tip: No slow cooker? No problem! Just poach the chicken instead. Place the chicken in a pot and cover it with water by about 2 inches; bring it to a boil over medium-high heat, then reduce the heat to low, cover, and simmer until cooked through, 8 to 10 minutes. Shred the cooked chicken with two forks. Add the chicken and cream cheese mixture to a baking dish; stir to combine and bake in a 425°F oven until heated through, about 15 minutes.

MEATBALLS WITH SPAGHETTI

Prep Time: 15 minutes **Cook Time:** 45 minutes
Soy-Free / **Serves 4**

Most of my upbringing was in Italy, where meatballs and spaghetti were served separately—never together as one meal. It wasn't until I was in sixth grade and having dinner at a friend's house that I had my first plate of spaghetti and meatballs combined. In this recipe I use ground turkey, but you could use ground beef or chicken instead.

1 pound ground turkey, preferably white and dark meat

1 small onion, finely chopped

1 garlic clove, finely chopped

½ cup rice cereal crumbs

¼ cup almond flour

½ cup unsweetened almond milk

1 large egg

2 tablespoons fresh parsley, chopped

2 teaspoons salt, divided

1 (24-ounce) can strained tomatoes

8 fresh basil leaves

1 (12-ounce) package gluten-free spaghetti

1. Preheat the oven to 400°F and line a baking sheet with parchment paper. In a large bowl, combine the ground turkey, onion, garlic, cereal crumbs, almond flour, milk, egg, parsley, and 1 teaspoon salt. Shape the mixture into 16 (1-inch) balls and place the meatballs on the prepared baking sheet. Bake until cooked through, about 15 minutes.

2. In a large saucepan, bring the tomatoes and basil to a simmer, stirring occasionally. Season the sauce with the remaining 1 teaspoon salt. Submerge the meatballs in the sauce, bring it to a simmer, and cook, covered and stirring occasionally, for 15 minutes.

3. In a large pot of boiling water, cook the spaghetti until al dente, about 15 minutes. Drain the pasta and toss it with the sauce. To serve, divide the spaghetti and meatballs among 4 shallow bowls.

Tip: To store, divide the spaghetti and meatballs evenly between two oven-safe storage containers. Cover them with tight-fitting lids and freeze for up to 1 month. To thaw, place the containers in the refrigerator overnight. Cover them with foil and bake in a 400°F oven until heated through, about 20 minutes.

SPICY SICHUAN BEEF WITH MIXED VEGETABLES

Prep Time: 10 minutes **Cook Time:** 15 minutes
Nut-Free, 30 Minutes or Less / **Serves 4**

Chinese food was unanimously my family's number one choice when dining out until my son Isaiah was diagnosed with gluten intolerance. I knew with some recipe testing I could re-create our favorite Chinese food dishes at home. One taste of this gluten-free Sichuan beef and you'll think you're dining at your favorite Chinese restaurant.

2 tablespoons olive oil, divided

1 pound beef stir-fry strips

2 tablespoons chili bean paste

1 tablespoon tamari

1 tablespoon rice vinegar

1 teaspoon sugar

½ teaspoon Chinese five-spice powder

1 carrot, thinly sliced

2 stalks celery, thinly sliced

1 garlic clove, finely chopped

1 scallion, chopped

2 jalapeño peppers, stemmed, seeded (if desired), and thinly sliced

4 shishito peppers

Salt

1. Heat 1 tablespoon of the oil in a large skillet. Add the beef and cook, stirring occasionally, until browned, about 10 minutes. Drain the beef on paper towels.

2. In a medium bowl, combine the chili bean paste, tamari, rice vinegar, sugar, and Chinese five-spice powder.

3. Using the same large skillet, heat the remaining 1 tablespoon oil over high heat. Add the carrot, celery, garlic, scallion, jalapeños, and shishito peppers. Cook the mixture, stirring constantly, until lightly charred, about 1 minute. Stir in the beef and the chili bean mixture. Cook for 1 minute and season to taste with salt.

Tip: If you can't find Chinese five-spice powder, you can make your own. Toast 6 whole star anise, 1 teaspoon whole cloves, 1 cinnamon stick, 2 teaspoons fennel seeds, and 2 teaspoons Sichuan peppercorns in a dry skillet over medium-low heat, shaking the skillet occasionally, until fragrant, about 2 minutes. Transfer the toasted spices to a coffee or spice grinder and pulse until finely ground.

MILLET, APPLE, AND DATE STUFFING

Prep Time: 20 minutes **Cook Time:** 40 minutes

Soy-Free / **Serves 8 to 10**

This stuffing has all the flavors of a late fall holiday table—apples, cranberries, and pecans. Millet, a naturally gluten-free grain, adds a buttery nuttiness to the dish, and the dates give a bit of sweetness to balance the tart cranberries.

2 tablespoons olive oil

1 onion, chopped

1 Golden Delicious apple, peeled, cored, and chopped

2 tablespoons fresh sage, finely chopped

Salt

Freshly ground black pepper

1 cup pecans, toasted and chopped

1 cup pitted dates, chopped

½ cup dried cranberries

1 cup millet

2 cups chicken broth

2 large eggs, lightly beaten

1. Preheat the oven to 400°F.

2. Put the oil in a large skillet and stir in the onion, apple, and sage. Cook over medium-high heat until softened, about 7 minutes. Season the mixture generously with salt and pepper. Stir in the pecans, dates, and cranberries and transfer the mixture to a large bowl.

3. Add the millet to the hot skillet and cook it over medium-high heat, stirring, until toasted, about 3 minutes. Add the broth and bring it to a boil over high heat. Reduce the heat to low, cover the skillet tightly with foil, and simmer until tender, about 20 minutes. Remove the pan from the heat and let the millet steam, covered, for 10 minutes. Fluff the millet with a fork.

4. Add the millet mixture to the apple mixture and season generously with salt and pepper. Add the beaten eggs and mix to combine.

5. Transfer the stuffing to a greased 11-by-7-by-2-inch baking dish. Bake, covered, until set, about 20 minutes. Then, remove the foil and broil until golden, about 3 minutes.

CHICKEN PESTO SALAD

Prep Time: 10 minutes **Cook Time:** 10 minutes
Soy-Free, 30 Minutes or Less / **Serves 4**

I grew up picking bunches of basil from our garden for my mom to use in pesto, which ultimately made its way into everything from pasta and soup to grilled corn and, of course, chicken salad. For a dash more flavor, try adding other fresh herbs like tarragon, dill, or chives.

2 pounds boneless, skinless chicken breasts
½ cup Basil Pesto (page 114)
½ cup mayonnaise

¼ cup sun-dried tomatoes, finely chopped
2 tablespoons finely chopped red onion
Little gem lettuce leaves, to serve

1. Place the chicken in a pot and cover it with 2 inches of water. Bring the water to a boil over medium-high heat, then reduce the heat to low, cover, and simmer until the chicken is cooked through, 8 to 10 minutes. When the chicken is fully cooked, remove it from the pot and shred it with two forks.

2. In a medium mixing bowl, combine the pesto and mayonnaise. Stir in the sun-dried tomatoes and red onions.

3. Combine the shredded chicken with the pesto mixture.

4. To serve, spoon the chicken salad into lettuce leaves.

Tip: Want to take this recipe to the next level? Stir some raisins into the chicken salad for a little sweetness.

Chocolate Chip
Oatmeal Cookies
Page 98

Chapter Eight

DESSERTS

EDIBLE COOKIE DOUGH

Prep Time: 10 minutes

Soy-Free, Vegan, 30 Minutes or Less / **Serves 4**

No need to worry about raw eggs in this unbaked cookie dough. In just minutes, you'll be indulging in a treat the whole family will love.

½ cup coconut oil, at room temperature

6 tablespoons packed brown sugar

6 tablespoons granulated sugar

3 tablespoons coconut milk

1 teaspoon pure vanilla extract

½ teaspoon salt

1 cup gluten-free oat flour

½ cup dairy-free chocolate chips

1. In a large bowl, use an electric hand mixer to beat together the coconut oil, brown sugar, and granulated sugar until fluffy, about 3 minutes.

2. Beat in the coconut milk, vanilla, and salt. Add in the oat flour ¼ cup at a time and beat until smooth. Fold in the chocolate chips.

Tip: Make this recipe your own by stirring mini marshmallows, chopped pecans, dairy-free peanut butter chips, or chopped dairy-free, gluten-free candy into the cookie dough.

BROWNIE BATTER BITES

Prep Time: 10 minutes, plus 30 minutes to chill
Soy-Free, Vegan / **Makes 16 to 18 bites**

Do you crave dessert right before bed? These no-guilt brownie bites are your sweet salvation. They also happen to be super quick to make. Double the recipe and freeze half for later—they'll keep for up to 1 month in a resealable container. The best part? You can eat them straight from the freezer. If the brownie batter dough looks dry and crumbly, add 2 tablespoons of water.

6 pitted Medjool dates

½ cup natural creamy almond or
   peanut butter

¼ cup unsweetened cocoa powder

1 teaspoon pure vanilla extract

⅔ cup gluten-free old-fashioned rolled oats

¼ cup coconut oil

3 tablespoons pure maple syrup

¼ teaspoon salt

2 tablespoons dairy-free chocolate chips

1. In a small bowl, soak the dates in 1 cup hot water for at least 5 minutes. Drain well.

2. Line a baking sheet with parchment paper.

3. Using a food processor or high-speed blender, combine the dates, almond butter, cocoa powder, vanilla, rolled oats, oil, maple syrup, and salt. Add the chocolate chips; pulse 3 times to incorporate.

4. Using a tablespoon, scoop out one heaping spoonful and roll it quickly with your hands to form a ball; place on the prepared baking sheet. Repeat with the rest of the batter.

5. Freeze until firm, about 30 minutes.

Tip: Have nut allergies? Swap in sunflower seed butter for the almond or peanut butter.

CHOCOLATE CHIP OATMEAL COOKIES

Prep Time: 10 minutes **Cook Time:** 10 minutes
Nut-Free, Soy-Free, 30 Minutes or Less / **Makes 18 cookies**

In this oatmeal cookie recipe, I swap chocolate chips for the classic raisins. You could also mix it up and stir in ¼ cup raisins or chopped pecans along with the chocolate chips.

½ cup non-hydrogenated shortening or
   8 tablespoons unsalted buttery stick,
   at room temperature
½ cup granulated sugar
½ cup packed brown sugar
2 large eggs
½ teaspoon pure vanilla extract

1 teaspoon ground cinnamon
½ teaspoon salt
½ teaspoon baking soda
⅔ cup Gluten-Free All-Purpose Flour
   (page 4) or store-bought blend
3 cups gluten-free old-fashioned rolled oats
½ cup dairy-free chocolate chips

1. Preheat the oven to 350°F and line two baking sheets with parchment paper.

2. In a medium bowl, cream together the shortening, granulated sugar, and brown sugar. Mix in the eggs, one at a time, until the mixture is smooth and creamy. Stir in the vanilla, cinnamon, salt, and baking soda. Gradually mix in the flour and oats until combined, then fold in the chocolate chips.

3. Drop spoonfuls of the cookie dough about 2 inches apart onto the prepared baking sheets; bake until golden, 10 to 12 minutes. Let the cookies cool on the baking sheets for 5 minutes, then transfer them to a wire rack to cool completely.

Tip: Love spice? Mix in 1 teaspoon ground cardamom.

SNICKERDOODLE-PECAN
ICE CREAM

Prep Time: 20 minutes, plus 2 hours to chill and 4 hours to freeze
Soy-Free / **Serves 4**

My favorite dairy-free ice cream is custard-based using dairy-free milk and eggs, which prevent ice crystallization and give the ice cream its smooth, creamy texture. This recipe is inspired by cinnamon-and-sugar-coated snickerdoodle cookies and classic butter-pecan ice cream. At Thanksgiving, I love to top a slice of pie—pumpkin or pecan—with this delicately spiced ice cream.

1½ cups dairy-free milk, preferably
   cashew, divided
3 tablespoons cornstarch
3 large eggs plus 2 large egg yolks, at
   room temperature

1 cup pecans, ½ cup finely crushed and
   ½ cup coarsely chopped
½ cup packed brown sugar
⅛ teaspoon ground cinnamon
⅛ teaspoon salt

1. In a small bowl, combine ½ cup milk with the cornstarch.

2. Place a large heatproof bowl over a pot of simmering water. Combine the eggs, egg yolks, crushed pecans, brown sugar, cinnamon, salt, and remaining 1 cup milk in the bowl. Whisk the mixture constantly and cook until steaming, about 5 minutes.

3. Whisk in the cornstarch mixture. Continue to cook while whisking constantly until the mixture is thickened, 6 to 8 minutes more. Let the custard cool slightly, then cover the custard surface directly with plastic wrap and refrigerate until cold, at least 2 hours.

4. Strain the custard mixture, pressing with a rubber spatula. After straining, pour the custard into an ice cream machine and process until it is the texture of soft-serve ice cream, 20 to 25 minutes. Stir in the chopped pecans. Transfer to an airtight container and freeze until firm, at least 4 hours.

Tip: Change up the recipe by stirring in dairy-free chopped chocolate or toasted coconut, or swirl in a nut butter while the ice cream machine is running.

Magic Creamy
Cilantro Dressing
Page 116

Chapter Nine

HOMEMADE STAPLES

BUTTER

Prep Time: 5 minutes, plus at least 30 minutes to chill
Soy-Free, Vegan / **Serves 4**

You can use this neutral-flavored, versatile dairy-free butter just as you would regular butter. That said, it's best used for low- to medium-heat cooking, since high-heat cooking (such as searing or frying) could cause the almond flour in the recipe to burn. This butter stores well in the freezer. Just pour the liquid butter into ice cube trays to make 2-tablespoon portions.

1 cup refined coconut oil

½ cup extra virgin olive oil

½ cup almond flour

1 teaspoon salt

½ teaspoon nutritional yeast

2 pinches ground turmeric

½ cup dairy-free unsweetened plain milk, storebought or homemade (page 107)

1 teaspoon apple cider vinegar

Put the coconut oil, olive oil, almond flour, salt, nutritional yeast, turmeric, milk, and vinegar in a blender; blend until smooth and creamy, about 1 minute. Transfer the butter to a resealable container and refrigerate for up to 2 weeks.

Tip: It's easy to customize this recipe to make various compound butters: Mix in garlic and finely chopped herbs like chives, basil, thyme, and oregano. Add in the garlic cloves during blending, then stir in the herbs.

EASY NUT OR SEED MILK

Prep Time: 5 minutes, plus 8 hours to soak
Soy-Free, 5-Ingredient / **Serves 4**

The dairy-free milks you find in your local supermarket are generally low in protein and made from tree nuts, which presents a big problem for those with nut allergies. The best part of this easy recipe is that you can choose your favorite nut or seed. My favorite way to prepare this for my son is using pumpkin seeds, with a pinch of cinnamon, a splash of vanilla, and a bit of maple syrup. The seeds or nuts are soaked overnight in water to soften them and improve their absorption, which results in creamier milk.

1 cup raw seeds or nuts   **4 cups water**
Salt

1. Put the seeds or nuts in a medium-size glass bowl and add 1 teaspoon salt and enough water to cover. Soak the seeds or nuts for at least 8 hours or overnight.

2. Drain and rinse the soaked seeds or nuts and put them in a high-powered blender along with 2 pinches salt and the water; blend until smooth and creamy, about 2 minutes.

Tip: Customize the recipe by blending in 1 tablespoon maple syrup or 3 pitted dates, ½ teaspoon pure vanilla extract, and ½ teaspoon ground cinnamon.

QUICK OAT MILK

Prep Time: 5 Minutes

Nut-Free, Soy-Free, Vegan, 5 Ingredient, 30 Minutes or Less / **Serves 4**

Oat milk is sweeter than nut or seed milks—even without added sugar. It bakes well and makes for a refreshing, drinkable milk. Be careful not to over-blend; if you process the milk for too long, you could get a slimy texture from the starch breaking down.

1 cup gluten-free old-fashioned rolled oats

3 cups water

½ teaspoon salt

½ teaspoon pure vanilla extract

1 pitted date

1. Put the oats, water, salt, vanilla, and date in a high-speed blender; blend until creamy, about 30 seconds. Using cheesecloth, filter the milk twice without squeezing the pulp.

2. Transfer the oat milk to a resealable container and refrigerate it for up to 5 days. Shake well before serving.

Tip: Give the milk a flavor boost: Blend in ¼ cup blueberries and 1 teaspoon ground cinnamon, or add an extra teaspoon of vanilla and 1 tablespoon maple syrup.

COCONUT WHIPPED CREAM

Prep Time: 15 Minutes, plus overnight to chill

Soy-Free, Vegan, 5 Ingredient, 30 Minutes or Less / **Serves 4**

This whipped cream works best when the can of coconut milk or cream is chilled upside-down overnight in the refrigerator, which lets more of the fat separate from the liquid. The tapioca flour in the recipe helps keep the whipped cream stable. Start with 1 tablespoon tapioca flour, and working 1 tablespoon at a time, add more until you reach a firm whipped cream consistency.

1 (14.5-ounce) can full-fat coconut milk, chilled upside-down overnight

1 teaspoon pure vanilla extract

¼ cup confectioners' sugar

1 tablespoon tapioca flour

1. Chill a large mixing bowl in the freezer for at least 10 minutes; scoop the firm part of the coconut milk into the chilled mixing bowl. With an electric hand mixer, beat the coconut fat on high speed until thick and creamy, 30 seconds to 1 minute. Add in the vanilla, sugar, and tapioca; beat on high speed for 1 minute.

2. Transfer the whipped cream to a resealable container and refrigerate for up to 1 week.

Tip: Save the liquid from your canned coconut milk for soups, smoothies, or as a replacement for water in sweet and savory recipes.

CREAM CHEESE

Prep Time: 10 minutes, plus 12 to 48 hours to ferment
Soy-Free, Vegan, 5 Ingredient / **Makes 2 cups**

Cream cheese has a quintessential soft, creamy texture and a wonderful tartness. Rather than adding lemon juice or vinegar, this recipe relies on fermentation for tartness. Bonus? You get a naturally occurring boost of probiotics. The ideal temperature for fermentation to occur is 80°F to 110°F—think of a turned-off oven with the light on or a warm room. Just make sure to avoid direct sunlight.

2 cups raw cashews, soaked overnight, rinsed, and drained
¼ cup dairy-free plain unsweetened yogurt

½ teaspoon salt
4 to 6 tablespoons water

1. Sterilize a 24-ounce glass container by carefully pouring boiling water over its entire surface, inside and out; drain, let cool to room temperature, and air dry.

2. Put the cashews, yogurt, salt, and 2 tablespoons of the water in a high-speed blender; blend until smooth and creamy, scraping down the sides as needed and adding water, 1 tablespoon at a time, to help the blades turn.

3. Pour the cashew cream into the sterilized container, cover it with cheesecloth, and secure the cloth with a rubber band. Place the container in a warm spot for 12 to 48 hours.

4. After the first 12 hours of fermentation, use a clean silicone spoon to taste the mixture for tartness and thickness; continue tasting every 8 hours until you reach your desired consistency. Cover and refrigerate for up to 1 week.

Tip: Make your own flavored cream cheeses by adding garlic and chives, jalapeño and scallions, or blueberries with a drizzle of maple syrup.

"GRATED" PARMESAN CHEESE

Prep Time: 5 minutes

Nut-Free, Soy-Free, Vegan, 5 Ingredient, 30 Minutes or Less / **Makes 1½ cups**

Mushrooms lend this recipe an umami flavor reminiscent of aged cheese. This Parmesan is precrumbled for easy sprinkling on your favorite pasta, salad, or for including in recipes like Basil Pesto (page 114).

¾ cup raw pumpkin seeds

1 teaspoon garlic powder

1 tablespoon nutritional yeast

½ teaspoon onion powder

3 ounces dried mushrooms

¾ teaspoon salt, plus more for seasoning

Put the pumpkin seeds, garlic powder, nutritional yeast, onion powder, mushrooms, and salt into the work bowl of a food processor; pulse until coarse crumbs form. Season with more salt if desired and store in a resealable container in the refrigerator for up to 2 weeks.

. . . .

Tip: Prefer nuts? Use cashews instead of pumpkin seeds for a smoother texture and a color that resembles regular Parmesan.

CREAMY RICOTTA

Prep Time: 5 minutes

Vegan, 30 Minutes or Less / **Serves 4**

Go ahead and stuff this ricotta into pasta shells, layer it between lasagna noodles, or serve it on crackers with summer tomatoes or your favorite jam.

1 cup slivered blanched almonds

½ (16-ounce) block firm tofu, drained
   and pressed

2 tablespoons freshly squeezed lemon juice

1 tablespoon gluten-free miso

½ teaspoon salt

1 teaspoon garlic powder

2 tablespoons olive oil

¼ cup water

1. Combine the blanched almonds, tofu, lemon juice, miso, salt, garlic powder, oil, and water in a blender or food processor; pulse until well combined.

2. Using a cheesecloth, filter twice without squeezing the pulp. Transfer to a resealable container and refrigerate for up to 5 days. Shake the ricotta well before serving.

Tip: No blanched almonds? Make your own: Boil whole raw almonds for 1 minute, drain and rinse under cold water, then squeeze the almonds to slip off their skins.

SLICEABLE TANGY MOZZARELLA

Prep Time: 10 minutes / Cook Time: 10 minutes, plus 2 hours to chill
Soy-Free, Vegan / **Makes 8 ounces**

Get ready to top your next pizza, chicken Parmesan, or minestrone recipe with this sliceable, stretchy mozzarella. The recipe uses oat flour and tapioca flour, which give the mozzarella its stretch.

1 cup soaked raw cashews

2 tablespoons sauerkraut

3 tablespoons sauerkraut juice

¼ cup water

3 tablespoons white wine vinegar

2 tablespoons gluten-free oat flour

1 tablespoon refined coconut oil, melted

2 tablespoons tapioca flour

¾ teaspoon salt

1. Combine the cashews, sauerkraut, sauerkraut juice, water, vinegar, oat flour, coconut oil, tapioca flour, and salt in a blender; blend until smooth and creamy, scraping down the sides of the blender as needed.

2. Pour the cheese mixture into a saucepan and cook it over medium heat, stirring constantly, until thickened, about 8 minutes. Transfer to a resealable container and refrigerate, uncovered, for at least 2 hours (until firm) before slicing; cover and store for up to 1 week.

Tip: Have a tree nut allergy? Replace the cashews with sunflower seeds.

BASIL PESTO

Prep Time: 5 minutes

Nut-Free, Soy-Free, 5 Ingredient, 30 Minutes or Less / **Makes 2 cups**

Spread this flavor-packed pesto on sandwiches and wraps, drizzle it over hot-out-of-the-oven pizza, or stir it into cooked pasta.

⅓ cup "Grated" Parmesan Cheese
    (page 111)
2 tablespoons raw pumpkin seeds
2 cups fresh basil leaves

4 garlic cloves
2 tablespoons freshly squeezed lemon juice
½ cup olive oil
¼ teaspoon salt, plus more for seasoning

Put the "Grated" Parmesan, pumpkin seeds, basil, garlic, lemon juice, olive oil, and salt in the work bowl of a food processor; pulse until coarse crumbs form. For a thinner consistency, add water 1 tablespoon at a time and pulse until your desired consistency is reached. Season to taste and serve, or store in a resealable container in the refrigerator for up to 2 weeks.

Tip: Swap in any leafy greens you have on hand, such as spinach, kale, Swiss chard, or mustard greens, for half of the basil.

CASHEW RANCH DRESSING

Prep Time: 15 minutes, plus 1 hour to chill **Cook Time:** 20 minutes

Soy-Free, Vegan / **Makes 2 cups**

With this nut-based version of iconic ranch dressing, you get all the creamy goodness with the added benefit of nutrient-dense cashews. You can use the dressing right away, but for the best flavor and texture, refrigerate for at least 1 hour.

1 cup raw cashews

½ cup cold water, plus more for simmering

1 tablespoon freshly squeezed lemon juice

¾ teaspoon apple cider vinegar

1 teaspoon dried dill

½ teaspoon dried parsley

½ teaspoon dried chives

¼ teaspoon onion powder

½ teaspoon garlic powder

¼ teaspoon salt

⅛ teaspoon freshly ground black pepper

1. In a small pot, combine the raw cashews with enough water to cover them by 4 inches. Bring the water to a boil over high heat, then reduce the heat to medium and simmer for 20 minutes. Drain and rinse the cashews under cold running water until cool. Transfer the cashews to a blender or food processor along with the cold water, lemon juice, and apple cider vinegar. Process until the mixture is smooth, scraping down the sides as needed.

2. In a small bowl, combine the cashew mixture with the dill, parsley, chives, onion powder, garlic powder, salt, and pepper; transfer the dressing to a resealable container and refrigerate it for at least 1 hour or, preferably, overnight. Store the dressing in the refrigerator for up to 1 week.

Tip: Be sure to use raw cashews—roasted nuts won't soften, resulting in more of a nut butter flavor.

MAGIC CREAMY CILANTRO DRESSING

Prep Time: 5 minutes
Soy-Free, 30 Minutes or Less / **Makes 2 cups**

Use this dressing as a dip for veggies, a dressing on chicken salad, or a crema-style sauce for tacos. The recipe works best with a thin, tart coconut yogurt; if using a dairy-free Greek yogurt, add 2 tablespoons of freshly squeezed lemon or lime juice to thin it.

2 tablespoons tahini

½ cup soy-free mayonnaise

½ cup dairy-free, soy-free unsweetened
   plain yogurt

1 bunch fresh cilantro leaves

2 jalapeño peppers, stemmed

½ teaspoon salt

¼ teaspoon freshly ground black pepper

1 teaspoon garlic powder

½ teaspoon onion powder

Combine the tahini, mayonnaise, yogurt, cilantro, jalapeños, salt, pepper, garlic powder, and onion powder in a blender and blend until the dressing is smooth and creamy, about 1 minute. If the dressing is too thick, add water, 1 tablespoon at a time, until your desired consistency is reached. Transfer the dressing to a resealable container and refrigerate for up to 10 days.

Tip: For a vegan option, swap in 1 medium pitted avocado and the juice of 1 lime for the mayonnaise. Refrigerate for up to 5 days.

CREAMY CHIPOTLE SAUCE

Prep Time: 5 minutes

Nut-Free, Soy-Free, 5 Ingredient, 30 Minutes or Less / **Makes 2 cups**

Slather this addictive chipotle sauce on everything from tacos to sandwiches and sweet potatoes to chili. If you don't need to omit soy, use whatever store-bought dairy-free yogurt and mayo you have on hand.

1 cup soy-free mayonnaise

1 cup dairy-free, soy-free unsweetened plain yogurt

1 (7.5-ounce) can chipotle peppers in adobo sauce, peppers finely chopped and 1 tablespoon sauce reserved

Juice of 1 lime

½ teaspoon ground cumin

Combine the mayonnaise, yogurt, chopped chipotle peppers, 1 tablespoon of adobo sauce, lime juice, and cumin in a resealable container; seal the container and shake it vigorously until the sauce is mixed well. Refrigerate for up to 2 weeks.

Tip: This sauce packs some heat. For a milder sauce, use half the amount of chipotle peppers, or omit them completely and just use up to 2 tablespoons of adobo sauce.

TEX-MEX STYLE QUESO

Prep Time: 5 minutes **Cook Time:** 20 minutes
Nut-Free, Soy-Free, 30 Minutes or Less / **Makes 2 cups**

This versatile queso goes with almost anything. A few favorite uses include mac and cheese, nachos, and burgers. You can swap pumpkin seeds for the sunflower seeds and paprika for the chipotle powder.

1 medium potato, peeled and quartered

1 medium carrot, peeled and chopped into 1-inch pieces

½ cup raw sunflower seeds

5 garlic cloves

2 teaspoons ground cumin

½ teaspoon chipotle powder

½ teaspoon onion powder

1 cup unsweetened dairy-free milk

½ cup vegetable broth

6 ounces jarred salsa verde or tomatillo salsa

½ cup chopped pickled jalapeño peppers plus 2 tablespoons juice

Salt

1. Put the potato and carrots into a medium pot and cover them with water by about 1 inch. Bring the water to a boil, lower the heat, and simmer, uncovered, until tender, about 10 minutes; drain the vegetables and reserve the pot.

2. Combine the cooked potatoes and carrots with the sunflower seeds, garlic, cumin, chipotle powder, onion powder, milk, broth, and salsa in a blender; blend until creamy, scraping down the sides as needed. Pour the sauce into the reserved pot, add the jalapeños with their juices, and simmer over medium-low heat until the queso is thickened slightly, 5 to 10 minutes; season with salt to taste. Transfer the queso to a resealable container and refrigerate for up to 1 week.

Tip: Speed things up by using an immersion blender to combine the drained, cooked potatoes and carrots in the pot with the sunflower seeds, garlic, cumin, chipotle powder, onion powder, milk, broth, and salsa.

MEASUREMENT CONVERSIONS

Volume Equivalents	US Standard	US Standard (ounces)	Metric (approximate)
Liquid	2 tablespoons	1 fl. oz.	30 mL
	¼ cup	2 fl. oz.	60 mL
	½ cup	4 fl. oz.	120 mL
	1 cup	8 fl. oz.	240 mL
	1½ cups	12 fl. oz.	355 mL
	2 cups or 1 pint	16 fl. oz.	475 mL
	4 cups or 1 quart	32 fl. oz.	1 L
	1 gallon	128 fl. oz.	4 L
Dry	⅛ teaspoon	—	0.5 mL
	¼ teaspoon	—	1 mL
	½ teaspoon	—	2 mL
	¾ teaspoon	—	4 mL
	1 teaspoon	—	5 mL
	1 tablespoon	—	15 mL
	¼ cup	—	59 mL
	⅓ cup	—	79 mL
	½ cup	—	118 mL
	⅔ cup	—	156 mL
	¾ cup	—	177 mL
	1 cup	—	235 mL
	2 cups or 1 pint	—	475 mL
	3 cups	—	700 mL
	4 cups or 1 quart	—	1 L
	½ gallon	—	2 L
	1 gallon	—	4 L

Oven Temperatures

Fahrenheit	Celsius (approximate)
250°F	120°C
300°F	150°C
325°F	165°C
350°F	180°C
375°F	190°C
400°F	200°C
425°F	220°C
450°F	230°C

Weight Equivalents

US Standard	Metric (approximate)
½ ounce	15 g
1 ounce	30 g
2 ounces	60 g
4 ounces	115 g
8 ounces	225 g
12 ounces	340 g
16 ounces or 1 pound	455 g

RESOURCES

Beyond Celiac: www.beyondceliac.org/about-beyond-celiac
For more than 15 years, Beyond Celiac has been the leading patient advocacy and research-driven celiac disease organization working to drive diagnosis, advance research, and accelerate the discovery of new treatments and a cure.

Bob's Red Mill: "Inside the Mill: A Guide to Going Gluten & Dairy Free."
www.bobsredmill.com/blog/healthy-living/a-guide-to-going-gluten-dairy-free

Celiac Disease Foundation: "Gluten-Free Foods." Accessed May 14, 2021. celiac
.org/gluten-free-living/gluten-free-foods
Since its founding in 1990, the Celiac Disease Foundation has funded and executed international initiatives in three principal areas to bring an end to the suffering caused by celiac disease: medical research, patient and healthcare provider education, and public policy advocacy.

Chebe: "Gluten-Free Resources." recipes.chebe.com/blog-gluten-free-resources
Originally started as a company that sells gluten-free and grain-free mixes, it now offers a website with many resources.

Gluten Intolerance Group: gluten.org
For over 46 years, Gluten Intolerance Group (GIG) has led the way in helping support your health and safety when it comes to living gluten-free.

Murray, Joseph. *Mayo Clinic Going Gluten Free: Essential Guide to Managing Celiac Disease and Related Conditions*. Chicago: TI Inc. Books, 2014.

Roehmholdt, Rachel. "Going Gluten and Dairy-Free for Beginners: Top 10 Tips." The blog of Rachel Roehmholdt.com. www.rachaelroehmholdt.com/top-1 0-tips-for-gluten-free-dairy-free-beginners

Schieffer, Josh. *2021 Gluten Free Buyer's Guide: Stop Asking Which Foods Are Gluten Free?* Self-published. 2020.

Up to Date: www.uptodate.com/contents/diagnosis-of-celiac-disease-in-adults
A Wolters Kluwer website that helps medical professionals make appropriate care decisions and drive better outcomes, UpToDate delivers evidence-based clinical decision support that is clear, actionable, and rich with real-world insights.

REFERENCES

Fleming, Alisa. 2020. "Non Dairy vs Dairy Free: Why One May Contain Milk."
GoDairyFree.org. Accessed May 12, 2021. GoDairyFree.org/ask-alisa
/non-dairy-vs-dairy-free.

US Food & Drug Administration. Last updated July 16, 2018. "Food Allergen Labeling
and Consumer Protection Act of 2004 (FALCPA)." Accessed May 12, 2020.
FDA.gov/food/food-allergensgluten-free-guidance-documents-regulatory
-information/food-allergen-labeling-and-consumer-protection-act-2004-falcpa.

US Food & Drug Administration. Last updated January 11, 2021. "'Gluten-Free'
Means What It Says." Accessed May 12, 2021. FDA.gov/consumers/consumer
-updates/gluten-free-means-what-it-says.

INDEX

V

W

X

Y

ABOUT THE AUTHOR

 **Silvana Nardone** is the author of several cookbooks, including *Gluten-Free Bread Baking for Beginners: The Essential Guide to Baking Artisan Loaves, Sandwich Breads, and Enriched Breads; Dairy-Free Meal Prep: Easy, Budget-Friendly Meals to Cook, Prep, Grab, and Go; The 30-Minute Dairy-Free Cookbook: 101 Easy and Delicious Meals for Busy People; Silvana's Gluten-Free and Dairy-Free Kitchen: Timeless Favorites Transformed;* and *Cooking for Isaiah: Gluten-Free & Dairy-Free Recipes for Easy, Delicious Meals.* She successfully launched Cooking for Isaiah® by Silvana Nardone, a gluten-free, dairy-free flour blend and baking mix company that gives gluten-free people the freedom to cook and bake again. Previously, Silvana was the founding editor-in-chief of celebrity chef Rachael Ray's magazine, *Rachael Ray Every Day*, and the owner of the cult Italian bakery, Fanciulla. She lives in New York City.

CPSIA information can be obtained
at www.ICGtesting.com
Printed in the USA
BVHW060814210921
617124BV00001B/1